who works with kids today. This book is like a glimpse into the future and a practical handbook all in one, showing us the incredible things that can happen when we choose to support and value the souls who are here to help us grow.
Shay Parker, Founder of Best American Psychics

What you hold in your hands is more than a book; it is a compass. In her gentle yet unwavering voice, Jackson guides you through the myths and mysteries of the rays, the science and soul-work of multidimensional living, and the real-life accounts of children whose very DNA pulses with cosmic codes.
Christopher B. Buck, Publisher of OMTimes Media

I0866371

Previous Books with ISBN

Mississippi Medium: My Journey from Southern Baptist to Talking to the Dead

ISBN: 978-0-578-56075-5

Secrets of the Secret

ISBN: 978-0-578-64041-9

Manifesting Your Magic in the 5D: Going Beyond the Laws of Attraction

ISBN: 979-8-218-47588-8

Manifesting Your Magic in the 5D (ebook edition)

ISBN: 979-8-9912708-7-8

Manifesting Your Magic in the 5D Workbook Journal

ISBN: 979-8-9912708-0-9

What People Are Saying About Children of the New Earth

This book is a profound and timely transmission that lovingly chronicles the arrival of our most radiant Starseed children. With reverence and clarity, it reveals the extraordinary gifts of the Rainbow, Diamond, Golden, and Solar Rays, and much more, and affirms what many of us have long intuited — that these children are here as master teachers, frequency holders, and living reminders of humanity's divine potential. Reading these stories feels like touching the future while remembering our deepest truths. A must-read for parents, lightworkers, and anyone committed to the awakening of the New Earth.
Maureen J. St. Germain, author of *Waking Up in 5D*

Children of the New Earth isn't just a book; it's a sacred transmission. A blueprint for understanding the radiant souls arriving now, encoded with frequencies that don't just challenge the old systems; they're here to completely rewire them. Jill M. Jackson brings their essence to life with reverence and clarity, honoring the truth many fail to see. These children didn't come to fit into this world; they came to build a new one. One rooted with a higher consciousness to help us remember what we have forgotten.
As a grandmother to one of these light-bearers, I know the frequency well. They are sensitive, wise, and pulsing with divine intelligence. This sensitivity they carry is not a flaw. It's their superpower. This book is a guide for the guardians. A compass for the keepers of these future architects. And a powerful reminder that what the world calls "too much" is exactly what makes them unstoppable."
Kim Russo, star of *The Happy Medium* as well as the long-running TV series *The Haunting of...* and *Psychic Intervention*

and author of *The Happy Medium: Life Lessons from the Other Side* and *Your Soul Purpose: Learn How to Access the Light Within*

Jill Jackson's latest book, *Children of the New Earth,* is an absolute necessity for parents and grandparents everywhere. As an Indigo child myself, I know how hard it can be to grow up without the support and understanding of those around you. As a parent to gifted children, I was able to experience the ease that comes with knowing and understanding the role of guardian of these sensitive and psychic souls. This book is a must-have, in my opinion, and I am so grateful that Jill was courageous enough to bring forth this information now, when it is so greatly needed in our world.
Sunny Dawn Johnston, Psychic Medium, Spiritual Guide, and Author of *Invoking the Archangels* and *The Love Never Ends*

I've been lucky enough to know Jill M. Jackson for 12 years now, and let me tell you, she's the real deal. She's completely dedicated to truth, to spirit, and to her special role as a guide connecting different realms. Her book, *Children of the New Earth: How Starseeds Are Shaping Humanity's Future,* is proof of just how gifted she is. She's not just a professional psychic medium and healer; she's a visionary, bringing us some seriously important wisdom for today. Jill has this amazing ability to take these almost otherworldly insights and make them practical and easy to understand. In this book, she gives us a helpful and caring guide for understanding and supporting the next generation of incredibly bright souls who are coming to Earth. Jill writes like someone who's been teaching for years, but with the warmth of a mother and the honesty of someone who truly lives what they preach. Her insights into Golden Ray children – and those yet to come – are not just interesting; they're a must-read for anyone

CHILDREN OF THE NEW EARTH

How Starseeds Are Shaping Humanity's Future

CollectiveInk

First published by Sixth Books, 2026
Sixth Books is an imprint of Collective Ink Ltd.,
Unit 11, Shepperton House, 89 Shepperton Road, London, N1 3DF
office@collectiveinkbooks.com
www.collectiveinkbooks.com
www.6th-books.com

For distributor details and how to order please visit the 'Ordering' section on our website.

ISBN: 978 1 917991 55 1
978 1 917991 56 8 (ebook)
Library of Congress Control Number: 2025947344

A CIP catalogue record for this book is available from the British Library.

Design: Lapiz Digital Services

UK: Printed and bound by CPI Group (UK) Ltd, Croydon, CR0 4YY
Printed in North America by CPI GPS partners

The manufacturer's authorised representative in the EU for product safety is: eucomply OÜ - Pärnu mnt 139b-14, 11317 Tallinn, Estonia,
hello@ eucompliancepartner.com, www.eucompliancepartner.com

CHILDREN OF THE NEW EARTH

How Starseeds Are Shaping Humanity's Future

By Jill M. Jackson

6TH BOOKS

London, UK

Washington, DC, USA

To my husband, twin flame, and best friend **D. Francis**:
Thank you for walking beside me in this lifetime, for your infinite belief in my mission, and for holding space along the way. Your devotion, grounding energy, and deep love have been the constant heartbeat beneath this sacred work.

To agent and publicist extraordinaire, **Gail Torr** of **Galaxy Media Management**:
Your belief in this book and your steady commitment to expanding its reach, has meant the world to me. Thank you for your encouragement, your instrumental feedback, and for pushing me to go deeper, both in what I share and in how I bring this work forward.

To the **Galactic Collectives** who generously channeled so much of what lives in these pages:
Thank you for trusting in me as a messenger, for your patience as I faced my own shadows, and for your higher vision. This book holds an encoded frequency within your cosmic downloads.

To the **parents, grandparents, and practitioners** who were interviewed:
You generously shared your stories, your wisdom, and your hearts—thank you. Your words brought tears, laughter, and those beautiful cosmic chills that remind us that Starseeds are here, and their light is already changing the world.

And finally, to the **Children of the New Earth**:
This book is to honor you. May these words stir the ancient knowing within, affirm the sacred courage you hold, and illuminate the brilliance of your light, as we build the bridge to the New Earth, side by side, soul by soul.

With deepest gratitude and love,
Jill M. Jackson

CONTENTS

CONTENTS

Introduction

The Prophecy

The year was 2014, and the events that unfolded were profound, and I certainly do not use this word lightly. As a psychic medium and channel, I am well-versed in strange and unusual occurrences. However, this was one of those times that shook my world in ways that took me years to understand fully.

As I settled into the familiar embrace of the room I had visited countless times, I took a deep breath and expressed my gratitude to the Universe for bringing Lucy and me together. Lucy, the owner and guardian of Altered Elements in Naples, Florida, offered an array of crystals and metaphysical supplies and created a stunning sanctuary for conducting classes and hosting events. This sacred and well-known refuge had witnessed my teachings on numerous occasions, as well as the delivery of messages from departed loved ones through private readings and group mediumship galleries. Naturally, it held a special place in my heart, a haven where I felt secure while recharging my own spiritual batteries. My heart swelled with emotion as I inhaled the rich scent of incense and connected with the exquisite healing properties of the crystals and gemstones thoughtfully arranged by Lucy throughout the room.

On that evening, Lucy would lead a group of twenty of us in a sound healing experience featuring crystal and Tibetan bowls, along with other instruments. As a bonus, she always offered a powerful meditation experience. While I allowed myself to ride the waves of vibrations from the instruments and Lucy's skillful hands, little did I, the psychic, understand how much that evening would forever change my life. A collective consciousness identified as The Emerald Group introduced themselves to me and subsequently transmitted a series of instructions throughout the remainder of the sound bath.

If I had not been in such a deep state of meditation, believe me, I might have surrendered to a full-blown tantrum, much like a toddler not getting their way. Sound familiar, anyone? For those of us who answered the call to awakening, there have been numerous occasions to vent our frustrations along the way. If circumstances had been different, this may have well been one of those opportunities for me to express myself in colorful language. Forgive me, I digressed. Let me get back to the reasons for the near tantrum. Firstly, I genuinely wanted to experience some semblance of normalcy as I immersed myself in a soothing sound bath and meditation. Secondly, I had been under the assumption that I was diligently on track in fulfilling my soul contracts. In a future chapter, I will delve deeper into the meaning of soul contracts.

Just as I had been doing for years, I was in Naples, Florida, dedicated to serving the Spirit world and clients in search of healing, guidance, or expanded knowledge. My busy schedule included teaching intuition and mediumship workshops, providing private sessions, and delivering mediumship messages to audiences through gallery-style readings.

Tonight was my night off, a self-care gift to replenish my energy. My "open for business" sign was off, and I had no intention of channeling. Nonetheless, as this stubborn Pisces has come to realize, Spirit always holds the ultimate wisdom. The transmission was obvious and very direct. I was told about a new breed of children coming in to assist Mother Earth. The Emerald Group introduced themselves and explained that I would be writing about these gifted kids and helping parents understand how to best parent these extraordinary humans. The Group told me that the first wave of Golden Ray children would begin incarnating in 2015. The download continued. These children have no karma as they have never had lifetimes on planet Earth. However, they are wise old souls, their wisdom culminating from millennia of lifetimes on other planets. Their most important mission is to anchor in Unity Consciousness on your planet. The downloaded transmission continued over the next several months, and new information continues to be spoken to me.

Those closest to me understand I seldom keep my feet firmly rooted on the ground. My friends and loved ones have become skilled at extending a loving, long-reaching hand to guide me back from the ethereal realms and bring me back into the physical world to join others.

However, this was different. The heightened energy signature from this interdimensional communication had me floating on cloud eleven. Much of my life is lived on cloud nine, so my holiday on cloud eleven was pretty darn cool! I was fortunate to enjoy this brief sabbatical for a few more hours, and I must admit, as I started to grasp the gravity of this mission, the plunge from cloud eleven back to planet Earth was undeniably jolting. I found myself lying on the ground looking upwards, wondering what the hell had just happened.

When I awoke the following day, I slowly felt the fear creep into the crevices of my mind. Human Jill, as I lovingly call my ego personality, immediately came up with many excuses for how this group consciousness must have the wrong Psychic Channel. "I wasn't even able to have my own children, and you want me to write a book about parenting gifted kids?" I heard myself arguing back. Their loving response, "*You chose not to bear biological children in this lifetime because you are to be a mother to many. In addition, you will be a surrogate Mother, if you will, assisting moms and dads along their path of awakening while teaching them how to embrace conscious parenting.*" The sweat began to form, and my heart started beating faster. "I know what will help me," I thought. "A double espresso caramel coconut milk latte always does the trick to help ease my worries." On the drive to the café, as my ego anchored in more fears, I relived some of the trauma I previously experienced, suffering five miscarriages and subsequently feeling manifestation failure from being unable to birth biological children.

I write about perceived manifestation failure extensively in my book, *Manifesting Your Magic in the 5D: Going Beyond the Laws of Attraction,* about soul contracts and the law of attraction. As further explained in my book, manifestation failure often stems from a false narrative manufactured by our egos when the Universe had plans for us that better aligned with our soul's purpose. Over the years, I have discovered the importance of putting my ego and fears in the spotlight, allowing them to feel acknowledged. Granting them a moment on the front and center stage enables my subconscious mind to unveil the intricate layers of these diverse fears. A common error we make is creating a narrative denying our fears' existence. By standing boldly in the spotlight, exposed for the world to see, we reduce the likelihood of burying our worries. Failure to acknowledge our fears can result in them being hidden and suppressed, only to resurface at the most inconvenient and unexpected moments.

While sipping my latte, I granted my ego the floor, allowing her to make her case and try to convince me that I might not be the right person for this mission. Fortunately, due to my extensive inner shadow work over the years, this storyline can be swiftly summarized in brief prose.

At the start of my awakening journey, I would write numerous novels in my head, elaborating on why it felt unsafe for me to embrace my authentic truth completely. Suppose you find yourself scripting your parables of excuses leading to personal disempowerment. In that case, I urge you to take a moment now to set an intention to condense them into concise short stories, embodying a plot of liberation and inspiration. Honestly recognizing our current positions along our journeys lays the foundation for constructing a more expansive reality.

As your foundation strengthens, it opens space to build bridges that can guide and assist others. Reframing in this way is a powerful tool for individuals responsible for nurturing gifted children. As I finished my coffee, I thanked my ego for showing up and speaking her mind. Yet, I affectionately reminded her that I had learned to trust in my Spirit Team over the years, and that was what I was intending to do now.

During my drive home, I reflected on the profound sense of love and support I experienced while immersed in the energy of the Emerald Group. Describing the unconditional love radiating from this multidimensional consciousness is difficult to express in words. As I surrendered to the tranquil, nurturing energy surrounding me, I explained to human Jill that once we returned home, she would play elsewhere so I could channel as much information as I needed for this brand-new assignment. Embraced by their energy and alongside my other Spirit Guides, I felt the beginning of courage and excitement seeping in.

I am sharing my vulnerabilities and fears, hoping to inspire others that we can handle whatever comes our way. If I can transform from the paralyzing fear of inadequacy that stems from not achieving biological motherhood and accept this sacred mission— you can also conquer your fears!

In Teddy Roosevelt's famous speech, he said, "The credit belongs to the man who is actually in the arena, whose face is marred by dust and sweat and blood; who strives valiantly; who errs, who comes short again and again, because there is no effort without error and shortcoming; who knows great enthusiasms, the great devotions; who spends himself in a worthy cause; who at the best knows in the end the triumph of high achievement, and who at the worst, if he fails, at least fails while daring greatly, so that his place shall never be with those cold and timid souls who neither know victory nor defeat."

As Brene Brown cleverly reminds us in her speeches, when she speaks about the concept of Daring Greatly. "I want to be in the arena. I want to be brave with my life. And when we make the choice to dare greatly, we sign up to get our asses kicked. We can choose courage, or we can choose comfort, but we cannot have both. Not at the same time."

I am so thrilled I chose courage over comfort. I have lost track of the times I have fallen from cloud nine, or even cloud eleven, and had my ass kicked along the way. However, this book was too important to keep from others. The blueprint provided to me by the Spirit World, intended for teaching others, stands as a much-needed guidepost in these unsettling and chaotic times.

The chapters in the book include all the categories of gifted kids, dating back to the 1800s and continuing through the present day. The characteristics of all types are covered, from the Indigos to the Crystal, Blue Ray, and Rainbow children to the Diamond, Golden Rays, and Solar Rays. These spirited and brave children incarnated to expand consciousness while educating humans about unity and heart coherence. The New Earth Children embody energy and frequency that people take notice of.

Many of you may already be familiar with Indigo Kids and Crystal Children. Most of you reading this book either identify with one of these categories or strongly suspect you do. It is essential to recognize that if you are a parent or guardian of a gifted child, you were chosen by them for this sacred assignment. Indeed, children do select their parents. I can already hear some of you rumbling, exclaiming, "There's no way in hell I chose my parents!" Rest assured; you did choose who would usher you into this lifetime.

Through the thousands of readings I have conducted, this revelation has remained a consistent message from those in the spiritual realm: Our souls incarnate in each lifetime to gain knowledge, evolve, and grow.

Depending on the specific growth opportunities we need in each lifetime, individuals from our soul groups and adjacent soul groups willingly step forward to incarnate as our parents, helping in our soul's development. There is a blueprint of sorts that each soul signs and consents to before embarking on its incarnation journey.

In specific readings, I have witnessed situations where a parent exercises their free will and deviates from the initial agreement. When this divergence from the original script becomes significant and sometimes even abusive, the soul who agreed to play the role as a child may choose to walk away and sever ties with that relationship. I cannot count the times in my mediumship readings when parents have come forward to admit and acknowledge that they veered off script and are sincerely apologetic. Years later, as I delved into Michael Newton's book, *Journey of Souls*, I was thrilled to find that the insights shared by his twenty-nine subjects under deep hypnosis mirrored the information I had gathered through my extensive mediumship sessions.

As you explore the chapters in the book, you will discover it is the Indigos, Blue Rays, and the Crystals who choose parents with tremendous lessons for soul growth. The Rainbow Rays have members who choose parents who need lessons, and others with more evolved and aware parents. The Diamond, Golden Rays, and Solar Rays will only choose parents and grandparents who are awake and supportive of their gifts. When I first dove into the soul assignment of these literary teachings, I planned to write the book entirely about the Golden Rays. However, during the psychic downloads and the interviews for the book, it became clear that fresh and added information was coming in regarding all the categories, and the book was beckoning to include all gifted Starseeds.

In addition, I have provided channeled information on how gifted kids and Starseeds have incarnated to help us understand and integrate artificial intelligence and transhumanism. As unsettling as these changes may feel at times, the reality is that they are upon us now. These special kids, especially the Diamond and Golden Rays, as well as the Solar Rays, are incarnated to assist humanity in this part of the Earth's evolution. As a bonus to this book, I unveil what the multidimensional groups have channeled to me about the next wave of kids who started arriving around 2020!

Throughout my life, I rarely felt as if I "fit in." Forget the cliched black sheep notion. At times, I felt as eccentric as if I were a carnival sideshow actor in the production of my own life. I can empathize with being unique. One of my most honored quests is to help ensure the new waves of gifted kids incarnating today will have the support and resources to embrace and celebrate their uniqueness. After all, their purpose is of the utmost importance in helping with our ascension and evolution, as well as the ascension of Mother Gaia.

Join me on the rest of the mystical journey through the book's pages, where I will share the profound insights I have learned about these extraordinary kids. Some of the material is from channeled downloaded information from group consciousness beings, some is from my own experiences as a natural born psychic medium, and the remainder is from real-life engaging stories from parents and grandparents of these special kids. This book was channeled and written for all of us to have a deeper understanding of the multitude of gifts children bring with them when they are born. Reading about each category of gifted children and adults offers us opportunities for personal growth.

Children of the New Earth focuses on the sacred role these children, who possess wisdom and knowledge not derived from their five senses or traditional modes of learning, are here to play. These young people carry codes within their DNA, which help humans open their minds to innovative thinking. This expansion paves the way to explore mysticism, ancient esoteric knowledge, and the multidimensional possibilities for humankind. Exploring the traits and personalities of each wave of gifted kids and adults brings a broader understanding of behaviors and the wiring of their brains. Who knows when the Universe will bring someone into your path, and you will be able to share this expansive knowledge with them!

Upcoming chapters will include detailed explanations of the rays, dimensions, and what ascension means. Before we dive deep into the categories, waves, or rays of the souls, I need to explain that each category's age range and years are not absolute. I have discovered that nothing or little in our reality is definite. Instead, it is an approximation. Many of the gifted kids fall on the cusp between categories. And much like astrological cusps, these kids inhabit traits of both types. The purpose of categorizing each ray is to provide an opportunity to understand the child and their gifts better. I will show how one child can be different from another in many aspects yet share similar psychic and physical abilities. I invite you also to enjoy the interviews, which include details and personal accounts of how extraordinary these kids are.

My spiritual journey as a Wayshower was inscribed in my soul contract before birth. My passions fully ignite when I explore the depths of spirituality and esoteric knowledge. Educating parents and guardians of gifted children is a tremendous aspect of my destiny. Having witnessed the spirit world and other nonphysical phenomena as a child myself gives me the empathy to understand how different many of these kids feel. My myriad paranormal experiences provide a container of expertise I am delighted and honored to share with other gifted kids and guardians who care for them.

It is my heartfelt prayer that you become infused with an energy of expansion as you read the material in this book. I wrote *Children of the New Earth* to bring healing and profound wisdom to everyone who reads it. Humanity needs fundamental and radical change. We are at a precipice in our Earth's evolution. It is time for all of us to understand that we survive our physical bodies and that when we expand our potential to the possibilities we agreed to in our soul's contracts, we cannot fit into the proverbial box any longer. Join me as we break free from the shackles of dogma and embrace the infinite possibilities of expansion.

Chapter 1

Wayshowers of Truth: The Rays That Light the Way

Unless you have been living under a rock for the past few decades, you are aware we are on a precipice of radical change. These times of change have been prophesied for years by many Native Americans, psychics, and channelers. However, to navigate these changes, innovation and out-of-the-box thinking are required. Are you familiar with the concept of old souls? Perhaps you have been told you are an old soul. They carry a deep wisdom of knowledge that transcends this current incarnation. Prior to any transformation, there must be an acknowledgement of the necessity for change. Without this awareness, the process of change becomes impossible. Old souls have an evolved soul, which means they possess the ability to recognize the need for growth and change, which is accompanied by an inherent desire to facilitate the needed changes. Old souls can draw upon a wealth of life experiences to accelerate the needed changes. If you find yourself recognizing the need for change, it is probable you are an old soul. However, if you recognize the need for change and then take action to pave the way for that change, you are a Wayshower.

Just as a Jedi utilizes a lightsaber, there are courageous pioneers wielding their galactic wands, opening portals to assist in universal expansion. These spiritual Jedi have a sacred mission to be a Wayshower of Truth. These trailblazers agreed on a soul level to fearlessly blaze the trail for others to follow. Though it took me many years to confidently wear the robes of a Pioneer, I now stand proudly within the truth of this honor.

When there is a sacred mission to shift paradigms, usher in revolutionary change, and evolve in exponential soul growth, pioneers are needed to facilitate this transformation. Chances are, if you have been drawn to read this book, you are either a pioneer in your own right, or you have been ignited within the flames of a Cosmic Ray. We will delve further into more intriguing information about Cosmic Rays later in the chapter.

What constitutes a pioneer? According to various definitions, the word "pioneer" indicates being the first to explore or settle or being a person or group that helps usher in a new way of thinking. Another characteristic of pioneers is their constant quest for knowledge—perpetual students and a lifelong desire to explore the deeper meaning and mysteries of life. Most pioneers embody respect for everyone's path, with this respect embedded deeply in their DNA.

Many of the pioneers and Wayshowers have faced quite a few life challenges. In other words, it is probable that your life path as a pioneer has not been an easy one. If you happen to know someone who has experienced a smooth and even charming life, it is likely that they are a newer soul. Newer souls tend to choose simpler life paths as a way of getting their feet wet, so to speak, before making a soul-level commitment to incarnate as pioneers. We progress as we navigate the challenges of life, and we acquire deep wisdom along the way. In my previous book, *Manifesting Your Magic in the 5D: Going Beyond the Laws of Attraction,* I delved into spiritual laws and soul contracts, focusing on the spiritual law of polarity and emphasizing the universal theme of balance in our world. There cannot be an inside without an outside, an up without a down, a light without a dark. There is a continuum of counterparts and opposites. All that exists does so on a spectrum, and one aspect cannot exist without the other.

If we never experienced pain, how could we genuinely appreciate bliss and joy? If you are an old soul, I would venture to say your spectrum of challenges and soul growth opportunities has seemed to be out of balance at times.

However, if we can recognize and accept that the joys and the trials are the same thing: life experiences, this awareness can help us navigate the path in a smoother way. Even though joy and pain are polarizations of the other, they are both needed for soul expansion. The complexity of this subject matter gives us a lot to consider and ponder. If we can rewire our brains to understand that we learn from our mistakes and that we become better humans after experiencing challenges, this will help us navigate our way with ease during times of strife.

The way to harmony with this spiritual law is to learn balance, and to appreciate the challenge of the extremes with detachment. Within every disappointment is the potential for greatness. True growth does not come from the challenges themselves; rather soul growth occurs based on how we react to the challenges. How do we learn to navigate our reactions with ease and grace? Through deep shadow work. We will explore this concept further in an upcoming chapter.

During the first channeled transmission about the new wave of gifted kids called the Golden Rays, it was downloaded to me that they would be traveling on the twelfth ray. Hearing the group talk about the twelfth ray was confusing at first as I was more familiar with the mystery teachings of the seven rays. Alice Bailey, Ernest Wood, and Madame Blavatsky each wrote of the seven rays. According to these teachings, every ray has a certain frequency and vibration.

In his Pranic Healing books, Master Choa Kok Sui states, "Understanding the Seven Rays gives you the ability to see people as they are ... By viewing individuals from various aspects and facets, your understanding deepens."

Humans are complex and multidimensional. We are comprised of our physical bodies, our mental bodies, our spiritual bodies, our souls, and our aspect of God/Source. Located outside of the physical body is what is called the aura. The aura is the field of energy that surrounds everything from living beings to inanimate objects. With the advent of Kirlian Photography, the aura can now be photographed. Closest to our physical body, only extending out about one to two inches in diameter, is what is known as the etheric aura. The astral aura is located outside the etheric aura and can extend anywhere from a few inches all the way to five feet or more depending on our emotional state. The aura can be seen in the astral body.

With practice, you can learn to control the astral aura and bring it closer to your etheric aura when more protection is needed from outside energy. In the upcoming chapter Medicine Bag of Mystical Gifts, I discuss how to teach children to work with their aura and how much they will benefit from learning this. At our retreats and workshops, this is one of the favorite exercises from the young Starseeds. Further insights into the aura will be provided in subsequent chapters, where we will delve into the characteristics of the rays and explore the distinct types of children associated with each specific ray.

It is my belief, which corresponds with the teachings of Bailey and Blavatsky, that humans possess opportunities to express aspects of one of the Rays. In *The Secret Doctrine,* H. P. Blavatsky introduced humanity to the concept of Rays. She describes the rays as impulses and taught that all beings arose from combinations of seven rays of God/Source. She further affirmed that the substance of our world—objective and subjective—is "spiritual," which is described as, "something beyond thought." Number seven is such a spiritual number rooted in layers of our history and conscious awareness. There are seven main chakras, seven days of the week, seven wonders of the world, the book of Revelation speaks of seven trumpets and seven seals, lucky seven on slot machines, and so forth. If the knowledge of the rays intrigues you, I highly recommend reading books by Blavatsky or Bailey. Ernest Wood wrote a summary of the original seven rays in 2010, titled *The Seven Rays: A Theosophical Handbook.*

I truly resonate with this spiritual teaching of cosmic truth, however, through my own connection to the higher realms, I became aware of more than seven rays. As the consciousness on our planet has increased, some psychic channels, including myself, began to recognize and integrate the higher rays into our awareness. The higher rays bring new energy, colors, vibrations, and cosmic codes. How exciting to now understand that we are aware of many more rays, and with these rays, we are offered a prism of varying degrees of human potential. As we continue to evolve and expand our awareness of frequency and vibration, a greater depth of wisdom and knowledge begins to seep into our being and reality.

As I channeled this innovative information, the excitement flowed through me like a river of possibilities. The ground-breaking transmissions and downloads given to me weave the original teachings of the rays into the tapestry of the New Earth Children and their sacred mission. If we can comprehend the fact that a pulse from a cosmic ray provides an opportunity for expansion, then we can expand on this concept in realizing that the New Earth Children carry an aspect of these cosmic codes within their very DNA. They carry and integrate dormant DNA and ascension codes within their physical vessels. The incredible transmissions downloaded to me explained that evolved Starseeds throughout various eras of Earth's evolution, agreed to incarnate, embodying one of the rays or aspects of the Creator. The aspects of the rays were brought into humanity in an order of semblance depending on the consciousness level of the era.

It is also important to note that when we discuss the energy behind each ray of consciousness, this does not mean that one ray is better than another ray. As humans, we still feel more comfortable looking at things in a linear way, or even a comparative manner. A theme from the multidimensional beings I channel is for humans to learn more fluidity. When we flow, we tend to have less rigidity. We learn to be nonjudgmental of those who are different than we are.

As we dive deep into the newly channeled information regarding each ray and the role the New Earth Children have played in history and will continue to play as Earth ascends and evolves, I invite you to open your heart to the knowledge and wisdom the rays teach us. Remember that within each of us throughout every incarnation, we choose to embody a ray of the Divine Creator. The brave New Earth Children agreed to incarnate together in waves to anchor in the teachings and wisdom of that ray, based on what humanity needed for soul evolution. The other important aspect that was channeled to me was this. The Starseeds embody a ray of consciousness, which has nothing to do with the plane or dimension of reality they originated. In other words, Starseeds from a multitude of dimensions and planets agreed to incarnate at the same time to anchor in a cosmic ray. For the purposes of the channeled material for this book, I will begin with the fifth ray.

Please understand that the corresponding dates downloaded to me may differ from what other authors or channels have previously provided. In the grand design, the dates are not as important as the embodiment of the characterization of the ray.

Fifth Ray: Known as the Emerald Ray

Frequency of color: Green

Date: 1800s

There were a few pioneers who chose to incarnate in the 1800s, bringing in the awareness of the fifth ray of consciousness with them. Frederick Douglass, 1818–1895, Susan B Anthony, 1820–1906, Harriet Tubman, 1820–1913, and Nikola Tesla, 1856–1943 are a few examples of Emerald Rays. When we refer to the channelings of Blavatsky, the fifth ray teaches us about scientific knowledge, justice, independence, and perceptive intellect. These four souls certainly embodied these traits.

Frederick Douglass, known for his outstanding orator skills, became one of the leading spokesmen for racial equality. Douglass was responsible for changing the minds and awareness of how many Americans viewed slavery.

Susan B Anthony became one of the most visible and outspoken leaders of the women's suffrage movement. Anthony was a frequent guest at Lily Dale, established in 1879 as a camp and meeting place for Spiritualists and Freethinkers. Do you recognize the coordination of threads in the tapestry, representing a deep and significant history and evolution? And to bring this example full circle, in 2023, Lily Dale hosted a Celebration of Women, highlighting the connection between spiritualism and the women's rights movement.

Harriet Tubman, known as "The Moses of Her People," escaped slavery, then courageously rescued countless slaves through her utilization of the underground railroad. A nurse for the Union Army during the Civil War, Tubman became the first African American woman to serve in the military of the United States.

Nikola Tesla, inventor extraordinaire, way before his "time," famously quoted "Let the future tell the truth and evaluate each one according to his work and accomplishments. The present is theirs; the future, for which I really worked, is mine." Tesla's quotes offer testimony that he was a New Earth Starseed.

Sixth Ray: Known as the Ruby Ray

Frequency of color: Red

Date: 1900–1950

Astonishing information recently channeled through me is regarding the Ruby Rays who incarnated on the sixth ray of consciousness. Spirit tells me the approximate range of Ruby Ray's incarnation dates is from 1900–1950. Their mission involves significant sacrifice, as they are prepared to endure substantial hardships for the benefit of others. Many Ruby Rays serve as spiritual warriors, acting as precursors to the arrival of the Indigos. A few examples are Mother Teresa, 1910–1997, Rosa Parks, 1913–2005, Nelson Mandela, 1918–2013, B. B. King, 1925–2015, Ansel Adams, 1902–1984, and Martin Luther King, 1929–1968.

Mother Teresa (1910–1997) may not have identified as a Starseed, yet her lifelong commitment to sacred devotion and humanitarian efforts clearly reflect the qualities of the Ruby Ry. Her dedication to aiding the poor and terminally ill significantly fostered empathy within humanity.

Rosa Parks (1913–2005) is a key figure in the American Civil Rights Movement. On December 1, 1955, in Montgomery, Alabama, she made history when she refused to give up her seat to a white man on a segregated bus, an act of defiance that ignited the Montgomery Bus Boycott. Parks' courage in the face of systemic oppression helped to challenge the deeply ingrained racial segregation laws of the time and became a symbol of resistance. Her actions were not just a personal act of protest but a catalyst for change, inspiring millions and contributing to the larger struggle for racial equality in the United States. Parks' legacy continues to resonate as a powerful example of bravery and the transformative impact of standing up for what is right.

Nelson Mandela (1918–2013) was a prominent figure who exemplifies an advanced soul, a Starseed with a mission to teach the world about forgiveness, tolerance, integrity, and compassion. He played a pivotal role in ending apartheid in South Africa and, despite enduring 27 years of unjust imprisonment, he emerged as a powerful symbol of unity and reconciliation.

B.B. King (1925–2015) was a musician known for his transformative impact on music and his dedication to authentic emotion and storytelling. His famous guitar, named Lucille, became a symbol of his personal journey and emotional depth, further illustrating his commitment to authenticity. Throughout his career, King used his platform to address social and racial issues. He broke barriers by achieving mainstream success during a time of racial segregation, advocating for equality and inspiring others to persevere despite adversity. This advocacy and dedication to promoting justice is consistent with the Ruby Ray mission of fostering sacred heart energy.

B.B. King often spoke about the spiritual aspect of music and its power to heal and transform. His performances were not just about entertainment but about creating a deeper connection with his audience and the broader human experience. This supports Ruby Ray's goal of expanding the heart from a grounded place, guiding transformation. King's impact extended beyond his lifetime, influencing countless musicians, and leaving a legacy in the blues and beyond. Like other Starseeds, who often serve as catalysts for future change, King's contributions continue to shape the music industry.

Ansel Adams (1902–1984) is widely known for his profound connection to nature, visionary approach to photography, and dedication to environmental preservation. Throughout his life, Adams was deeply involved in environmental activism, tirelessly advocating for the protection of natural landscapes. His stunning photographs not only captured the grandeur of nature but also served as powerful calls to action for conservation.

Adams embodies the traits of a Ruby Ray through his visionary artistry, profound environmental commitment, and intuitive connection to the natural world. His legacy continues to inspire awe and introspection, encouraging a deeper appreciation of the beauty and importance of preserving our planet.

Martin Luther King Jr. (1929–1968) was a visionary leader and one of the most influential figures in the American Civil Rights Movement. Known for his unwavering commitment to nonviolence and equality, King led peaceful protests and delivered powerful speeches that called for an end to racial segregation and injustice. His most iconic moment came with the "I Have a Dream" speech during the 1963 March on Washington, where he articulated a vision of a world where people are judged by the content of their character, not the color of their skin. King's leadership and dedication to justice helped galvanize the movement, leading to significant legislative changes, including the Civil Rights Act of 1964 and the Voting Rights Act of 1965. His legacy lives on as a symbol of hope, unity, and the enduring fight for civil rights.

According to Blavatsky's transmissions, the sixth ray of consciousness represents ministry, devotion, self-sacrifice, and tolerance. Whether you personally agree with the views or teachings of those listed above, we can certainly appreciate the sixth ray pulses of purpose that each one incarnated within. When you read about the Diamond Rays, you will recognize the similarities within the energies of these rays. The energetic signature of the Ruby Ray is quite different than the energy of the Indigo Ray, better known as the Indigo Children.

Rays seven through thirteen are each covered in separate chapters of the book. Fresh and new insights from each ray of consciousness represented by the New Earth Children have been downloaded to me and I am overjoyed to share these contemporary transformational philosophies with you.

Seventh Ray: Known as the Indigo Children

Frequency of color: Violet or Purple

Date: 1950–1990

The term "Indigo Children" has gained widespread recognition, although sometimes inaccurately applied to all gifted children. Indigos embody the energy of the seventh ray of consciousness and are known for their unconventional thinking, often challenging established religious and governmental norms. In Chapter 2, you will find a wealth of new information, along with fascinating interviews featuring adult Indigos. As an Indigo myself, the upcoming chapter holds special significance, and I look forward to sharing my firsthand experiences and stories.

Eighth Ray: Known as the Blue Ray Starseeds

Frequency of color: Blue/Green

Date: 1950–2005

The Blue Ray Starseeds arrived on the eighth ray of consciousness and sometimes have an aquamarine aura. In chapter 3, we uncover their unique mission of teaching humanity about the high heart. These special light workers are here to anchor in the reality that we can speak our truth from a place of love, rather than a place of anger.

Ninth Ray: Known as the Crystal Ray Starseeds

Frequency of color: Crystalline/Quartz

Date: 1985–2005

The Crystal Children arrived embodying the energy of the ninth ray of consciousness, offering humanity a gentler way of ushering in change. In Chapter 4, we will explore the vast differences between the Indigos, Blue Rays, and the Crystals, while demonstrating the powerful examples of expansion offered by all three rays.

Tenth Ray: Known as the Rainbow Children

Frequency of color: Chakras/Colors of the Rainbow

Date: 2005–2015

The Rainbow Children incarnated on the tenth ray of consciousness and have the distinctive ability to inhabit the energy of numerous rays shown through their aura which sometimes looks like a rainbow. Those born as a Rainbow Child will anchor the balance of divine feminine and divine masculine and how this relates to ascension. When we understand the role Rainbow Children are incarnated to play, it is not surprising to consider the popularity of the transgender rights movement over the past decade. In chapter 5, you will develop a deeper understanding of these kids through the amazing firsthand interviews.

Eleventh Ray: Known as the Diamond Rays

Frequency of color: Silver/Pink

Date: 2010–2020

The Diamond Children, arriving on the eleventh ray of consciousness exhibit purity and innocence while weaving in layers of multidimensional wisdom. They are the final wave of children who chose to incarnate with the mission of helping humanity heal. The generations that follow carry a new directive, one focused on healing Mother Earth and continuing to build bridges to the New Earth. In chapter 6, we will read more about their fascinating abilities through personal stories and accounts from Diamond Ray Guardians.

Twelfth Ray: Known as the Golden Rays

Frequency of color: Gold

Date: 2015–2025

As detailed in the introduction about my prophecy of this ray of children, the Golden Rays hold a special place in my heart. Arriving on the energy of the twelfth ray of consciousness, these exceptional kids are here to help anchor in Unity Consciousness while helping Mother Earth in her ascension. Chapter 7 offers amazing interviews with parents and grandparents of Golden

Rays as well as new downloads transmitted to me regarding their special role in helping humanity begin to understand artificial intelligence.

Thirteenth Ray: Known as the Solar Rays

Frequency of color: Gold/Orange

Date: 2020–2030

Ray thirteen represents new channeled information given to me about the wave of children who began incarnation after the Golden Rays. This breed of prophesied children will embody the rhythms of The Central Sun and will help bring new innovations surrounding sustainability. These Starseeds do not arrive from the physical Sun, but rather the multidimensional, spiritual Sun at the heart of all life. Chapter 8 will examine the energy present within their DNA, which will activate latent codes in many twin flame souls who have incarnated concurrently at this time. This activation will further establish the equilibrium of the Christ Consciousness energy and the Sophia Consciousness energy.

***

Throughout the book you will discover my theories on ascension, both an individual soul's ascension as well as Mother Earth's ascension. What I have come to understand through the patient teachings from Spirit, is that the ascension process is not a destination or a locale, it is an integration of various aspects of the God/Creator's rays within the physical representation of our souls.

Since energy cannot be created or destroyed, and quantum physics has shown that everything within our reality is interconnected, it can be inferred that the ascension process involves planetary changes as well. Mother Earth's ascension is intricately connected to our expansion.

You will also notice that I refer to density and dimensions at several instances throughout the remainder of the book. Density, in its simplest form, means a measurement within a particular unit. Those of us who channel multidimensional beings will sometimes use the word density to convey the delta between the degree of separation. For example, as you travel from the higher density to a lower density, a degree of separation entails. Dimensions are not physical places, rather they are levels of consciousness. The third dimension is dense and filled with duality, division, and separation, while the fifth dimension begins to incorporate non-duality, oneness, and unity. The New Earth Children incarnating on the rays of consciousness bring with them a soul mission to activate the awareness of expansion, evolution, and the embodiment of the New Earth paradigm.

All the New Earth Children from every ray are pioneers, visionaries, or Wayshowers. They are nonconformists and yield a fierce and courageous spirit. They sing the song of freedom and dance to the beat of their own drums. Most of these children feel a stronger connection to the spirit realm or galactic realm than they do residing in the realm of the norm. For most people, they can relate to the famous Forrest Gump Quote, "Life is like a box of chocolates, you never know what you're going to get." – However, life for Starseeds is more like chocolatier Willy Wonka exploring a chocolate factory nobody else can even see! The proverbial metaphor for someone looking at you as if you have three heads, becomes a well-worn hat for Starseeds. I recall one of those three headed moments I experienced personally.

It was a warm, humid day in the deep south, and I remember basking in the normalcy of watching a baseball game being played. As I am sitting in the bleachers amongst the other spectators, watching my nephew play outstanding baseball, out of the blue, a few wasps start flying around the people sitting in the stands. Panic began to arise, as heads began to bobble up and down to stay out of the path of the stinger. Without a thought in my head, I stood up and started sweet-talking to the wasps. I had entered an altered state as I had done so many times before and began to merge my energy with the energy of the wasps. I heard myself instructing the crowd to begin their own flattery and praise in a language the wasps could understand. After all, the southern charm of "bless your little heart" should certainly be transferable to a winged insect! As I watched the wasps fly away, and subsequently started to feel my human awareness of Jill coming back into my body, I opened my eyes to witness everyone in the stand looking at me as if I were auditioning for the lead psychopath in the next *Silence of the Lamb*s movie. The shock on everyone's face eventually turned to hysterical laughter and I laughed with them as I quietly took my seat to watch the remainder of the game. I am positive that quite a few of you Starseeds can relate to consistently feeling like a fish out of water. These reminiscences bring me to another matter important for New Earth Children and their guardians to understand.

While it may seem exciting and thrilling to witness a Wayshower of Light bravely blazing the trail for others to follow, the reality is a mixed bag of candy. Some days, as a pioneer you feel like a sweet candy that everyone loves and savors. Other days, you realize that those around you are recoiling as if you were the sourest candy that they had to spit out of their mouths. Ouch!

If you or your child carry the badge of Wayshower, there are those who will be repelled by the frequency emanating from the auric field. Sadly, there may even be those who try to destroy the messenger of the mission. In a subsequent chapter, we will explore ways to recognize lower vibrational energies that bully those who are different, as well as tools to armor and protect these brave gentle warriors who selfishly agreed to bring new cosmic energy to humanity.

As mentioned previously, the intent is not to try and put all New Earth Children in the same box. The purpose is to create a better understanding of their beautiful differences, so we can celebrate diversity. Knowledge creates expansion and tolerance. Expansion paints a canvas of acceptance, compassion, and kindness, which is exactly what our New Earth Children will need to not only survive but to thrive and flourish on their sacred missions.

Chapter 2

The Journey of Indigo Souls: Warrior Spirits of Change

Indigo's rode in on the seventh ray of consciousness, shaking things up like a twister auditioning for the *Wizard of Oz*. The characterizations can be complex and multifaceted, like a yellow diamond in the rough. While traits like strong-willed and fiery temperaments often characterize Indigo individuals, it is important to note that not all Indigos advocate for change through aggression. Indigos, such as John Lennon and Princess Diana, exemplify how change can be brought about through their passion and energy. Princess Diana illustrated this through her compassionate heart and loving nature, while still facilitating a wave of awakening to new possibilities. Lennon illuminated our minds through thought-provoking lyrics, clearly creating friction with their stimulating songs.

Most indigos were born between 1950 and 1990, recognizable by the hues of indigo, violet, or deep blue in their aura. These individuals possess a profound clairvoyance that extends years into the future, offering a glimpse of the possibilities that emerge when humanity embraces diversity instead of division.

Nancy Ann Tappe, creator of the indigo revolution, incarnated on the Ruby Ray in 1931. She originally coined the term "Indigo" in the late 1960s, and it gave birth to a movement that established the foundation for viewing certain aspects of humanity through a colored perspective. Despite the accidental discovery of Kirlian Photography in 1939, Nancy was the pioneer in linking psychic and empathic abilities to the color of one's aura. In Chapter 1, we established a solid foundation for a comprehensive understanding of the profound mission of the Indigos and their role as visionaries and Wayshowers.

As revealed in the previous chapter, there were earlier pioneers who incarnated before the indigos, who rode in on the sixth ray of consciousness. Rosa Parks and Martin Luther King traveled on this ray in 1913 and 1929, respectively. They each offered a glimpse of possibilities that emerge when humanity embraces diversity instead of division and adopts love over hate.

If you feel a spark of curiosity and wonder whether you might be an Indigo, let us explore the key traits that define this unique soul group.

Nonconformist and Old Souls

Indigos do not fit into the norms of society. Many of them understand at an incredibly early age that they are quite different. Below is an illustration from an interview with Indigo Michael, born on March 4, 1954.

Michael explains, "You know, I honestly cannot remember a time when I *did* think inside the box. It just never really fit me. I always felt ... different. Like an odd duck, I suppose. And as I got older, it became more obvious to me and to my parents. They really did not know what to do with me. I will tell you this: there was this one moment back in third or fourth grade that has always stuck with me. I was a huge science fiction fan at the time, so that had something to do with it. But I remember sitting there and suddenly thinking, *"What if I'm the only real person here ... and everyone else is a robot?"*

Yeah. That thought just hit me out of nowhere. But here is the thing, it did not feel weird to me. Not at all. It felt ... like a message. Like a quiet knowing that I was not really *from here*. And looking back, it was just the first time I started waking up to the idea that a lot of people around me were living in something like ... the Matrix. You know? Just going through the motions."

Sally Rice, Psychic Medium and Indigo Ray Starseed, bursts into laughter as she shares, "I've always been a vocal nonconformist!"

Champions of Fairness, Justice, and Equality

Indigos have a deep knowledge that they are here at this time in human history to be effective in heralding transformation, however, a vast difference between the Indigos and future generations of gifted children is how strong willed and determined they are. The Golden Rays are also strong willed, but we will explore this trait of Golden Rays in the Golden Ray chapter.

Indigos often challenge traditional societal norms and may rebel against authority, especially when they perceive rules as lacking fairness, justice, or integrity. Speaking as an adult Indigo, I have always felt a deep connection to equality, fairness, and justice—these principles have consistently guided the causes I have been passionate about. It has been hard for me to understand how others can witness inequality and injustice without feeling frustrated or even outraged.

I vividly recall a moment of gender inequality I experienced in my twenties while working as an assistant controller in a professional environment. An upper-level executive informed me that I was one of about ten women chosen to greet visiting male executives at an upcoming conference. His exact words were, *"Don't worry, all you need to do is put on a tight white shirt, a short black skirt, and stand there looking pretty."*

My Indigo instincts kicked in immediately, and I could not let it slide. I responded, *"How many men did you choose to stand there and look pretty in provocative clothing?"* The look on his face was priceless. I declined his offer and communicated that I had not spent five years in college to take on a purely decorative role. I noted how troubling it was that only women had been chosen for this task.

Determined to take a stand, I rallied the other women involved and encouraged them to reject this demeaning request. While they initially agreed, when the time came to speak up, I found myself standing alone. The others had chosen to remain silent out of fear of losing their jobs. At the time, I found their decision frustrating and disappointing, but I have since recognized that not everyone is inclined to challenge authority. Unless you incarnate with the seventh ray of Indigo energy, standing up to such blatant injustice may not come naturally.

A few weeks later, I was fired from my position. Undeterred, I filed a lawsuit against the organization for its discriminatory practices. I am proud to say that my courage led to pioneering changes in their policies regarding women's rights. Looking back, I was so young, still discovering my gifts and trying to understand why I felt so different from others. Yet even then, I knew this: it was in my DNA to stand up for what was right. For me, there was no other choice.

Indigo Michael recalls: "I have always had a keen sense of justice and injustice, as far back as I can remember. It is all about right and wrong, good, and bad. I latched onto that from an incredibly early age. I was a Star Trek fan from the very first show. I admired William Shatner and the role he played as Captain Kirk. Fortunately, my dad was deeply committed to civil rights, so I was exposed to those values early on, especially in relation to the civil rights movement. I was hungry for knowledge and wisdom from a noticeably young age."

Sally continues, "I am a defender of justice and equality. When I see dishonesty or fraud, I simply cannot stay silent. I speak out with intensity because truth matters."As she reflects, Sally shakes her head in disbelief at how many choose silence in the face of injustice. Her path, however, has always been guided by courage and clarity.

Sensitive to Chemicals and Advocates for Environmental Causes

Another Indigo trait is an increased sensitivity to chemicals and environmental disturbances that others tolerate with ease. Many Indigos are passionate advocates for environmental causes, often going to great lengths to challenge unethical corporations and individuals.

Erin Brockovich, born in 1960, is a remarkable example of a brave Indigo. While working as a legal assistant at a law firm, Erin uncovered medical records that piqued her curiosity. Through her relentless investigation, she connected these records to toxic contamination caused by Pacific Gas and Electric's negligent waste disposal practices. Teaming up with attorney Ed Masry, Erin spearheaded a class-action lawsuit on behalf of the residents of Hinkley, California, who suffered serious health consequences due to PG&E's actions.

Her unwavering efforts led to a groundbreaking $333 million settlement, one of the largest direct-action settlements in U.S. history. This victory not only brought justice and compensation to the affected residents but also spotlighted the importance of environmental and corporate accountability.

Today, Erin remains a fierce advocate for environmental and consumer issues, focusing on cases of water contamination and public health threats. Her story is a shining example of how determination, courage, and a deep sense of justice, the hallmarks of the seventh-ray Indigo energy, can drive meaningful change.

If you have not seen the 2000 Erin Brockovich film, starring Julia Roberts, it is a powerful depiction of this historic fight for environmental accountability, and I highly recommend watching it.

Intuitive and Clairvoyant

Many Indigos have spent years navigating the unique experience of knowing or sensing things before they happen, a gift often misunderstood by others. Some possess the ability to perceive aura and energy fields, enabling them to instantly assess whether someone is trustworthy. While they may be labeled as judgmental for distancing themselves from certain individuals, with time, wisdom, and a deeper understanding of their gifts, they come to recognize this discernment as a vital tool for self-protection. This discernment allows them to safeguard themselves from those lacking integrity and honesty.

The color Indigo significantly amplifies their clairvoyance, enhancing their ability to foresee future events. However, many Indigos wrestle with the challenges of their prophetic insights, especially when their visions predict difficult or negative outcomes. This often brings the tricky question: "Do I share these visions, or do I remain silent?" Through mentoring others with clairvoyant and psychic abilities, I have come to understand that this decision must be deeply personal. Everyone must carefully consider the impact of their insights and choose how to use their gifts in alignment with their intuition and purpose.

Sally explains, "From a very young age, my psychic gifts were undeniable, visions of future events were shown, I connected with other realms, and the unmistakable knowledge of what is real and true was clear."

Sally describes her gift as seeing threads of light that others might miss. "I recognize patterns, and through clairvoyance, I see the truth emerge," she explains with quiet certainty. "My readings are not about telling people what they want to hear, but about illuminating what their soul already knows."

I have personally known Sally for many years and in her presence, one feels both the fire of her conviction and the calm of her vision. Sally Rice is not just a psychic medium, she is a voice for truth, justice, and awakening.

When gifted with the abilities of prophecy and clairvoyance, our intention is never to instill unjust fear in someone's life. However, there are moments when a clairvoyant psychic can offer warnings about potential challenges or difficult events. We have all heard stories of individuals who, through clairvoyance or even claircognizance, knew how to avoid a particular situation, such as not boarding a plane that later crashed.

It is one of my passions to teach ethics and responsibility when it comes to clairvoyance. In truth, I have stepped onto my metaphorical soapbox countless times to advocate for this cause. I can easily identify an untrained psychic, much like spotting someone wearing a yellow shirt in a room full of people dressed in black. I have heard stories of gifted children innocently exposing secrets. Although young children may be excused from this behavior, understanding professional ethics in clairvoyance is crucial. Learning and applying these ethical guidelines ensures that their abilities are used with respect and responsibility.

Labeled Conspiracy People

The Indigo Revolution paved the way for prominent whistleblowers, some of whom have been labeled as conspiracy theorists. Just as Harriet Tubman's courageous efforts in the 1800s were known as the Underground Railroad, these Indigos, born with a strong purpose to expose secrecy and corruption, harnessed the "underground railroad" of the internet—the World Wide Web.

Julian Paul Assange, born in 1971, exemplifies the traits of an Indigo, driven by a mission to reveal truth and challenge secrecy. He is best known as the founder of WikiLeaks, an organization he launched in 2006 to publish classified, censored, or otherwise restricted information of public significance, often sourced from whistleblowers.

Supporters see Assange as a champion of free speech, government transparency, and the protection of whistleblowers. On the other hand, critics argue that WikiLeaks' actions have endangered national security and the safety of individuals identified in its disclosures.

Whether viewed as a hero or a provocateur, there is no denying that Julian Assange remains a polarizing figure. His work with WikiLeaks has ignited global conversations about the delicate balance between transparency, privacy, and security, as well as the responsibility of journalists and publishers in holding powerful institutions accountable.

Edward Joseph Snowden, born in 1983, is renowned as a whistleblower who, in 2013, unveiled classified information from the U.S. National Security Agency (NSA). His revelations exposed global surveillance programs conducted by the NSA in collaboration with other governments and telecommunications companies, igniting worldwide debates about privacy, government overreach, and the limits of national security.

Whether one aligns with Snowden's actions or not, it is undeniable that his disclosures led to significant reforms, including the enactment of the USA Freedom Act in 2015, which curtailed mass data collection practices. His revelations have fueled ongoing conversations about the importance of whistleblower protections and the delicate balance between safeguarding national security and preserving individual privacy.

Much like Julian Assange, Snowden is a polarizing figure. Supporters view him as a courageous patriot who stood against government overreach, while critics label him a traitor who jeopardized national security and lives.

Regardless of individual opinions on their methods, both Snowden and Assange have played pivotal roles in expanding humanity's conscious awareness, offering transformative and thought-provoking insights into the hidden workings of powerful institutions. These brave souls and others laid the groundwork for the creation of friction to open awareness within humanity.

Creative and Visionary

Indigos often express themselves through art, music, writing, or other forms of creative endeavors and think freely. The seventh ray of consciousness delivered many examples of Indigos who became famous based on their contributions to the expansion of consciousness and the expression of that awareness.

John Lennon (1940–1980) left humanity a timeless legacy of songwriting and lyrics filled with provocative, thought-provoking ideas that challenged conventional thinking. Lennon is an example of a Starseed on the cusp between Ruby Ray and Indigo. He carries energy from both rays yet is an example of the first wave of Indigos. He exemplifies the qualities of an Indigo through his visionary nature, rebellious spirit, and unwavering commitment to peace and love.

A proud nonconformist, Lennon was driven by a deep sense of purpose to inspire change. His resistance to societal norms is evident in his outspoken critiques of war, materialism, and social injustice, embodying the Indigo trait of questioning and dismantling established systems. His vision of a world without division, inequality, or suffering reflects the Indigo mission of elevating collective consciousness and fostering global transformation.

John Lennon's life and legacy encapsulate the essence of an Indigo: a revolutionary soul with an unshakable belief in a better world, who used creativity, authenticity, and fearless activism to uplift humanity and ignite meaningful change.

In my book *Mississippi Medium: From Southern Baptist to Talking to the Dead,* I share my personal experience with John Lennon. One day, while sitting on my yoga mat in our Healing Center, I noticed a face on the hardwood floor. You would think I would be used to this by now! Still, I closed my eyes to clear my vision, thinking I might simply be "seeing things." When I reopened them, the face remained—a clear image of John Lennon peering out at me through his iconic round glasses.

John Lennon, like many gifted musicians who were tragically murdered, continues to work through mediums and psychics like me to bring knowledge about the evolution of consciousness through awareness. His presence was both humbling and thrilling, as he lent his energy to support my mission of bringing light to these important truths.

Music and lyrics hold a profound power to influence energy and vibration. Through my work with sensitive and gifted children, as well as their parents, I emphasize how music can be a transformative tool for shifting energy. John Lennon's connection reminds us of the extraordinary impact music can have on our collective consciousness.

Empathetic and Sensitive

Indigos, like other categories of New Earth Children, are deeply empathetic and can easily become overwhelmed by the emotions of others or the collective energy they tune into.

In my intuitive development programs, I guide individuals in recognizing whether an emotion they are experiencing is their own or if it belongs to someone they have been around. I also emphasize the importance of setting healthy boundaries and protecting the energy field and aura for sensitive individuals. To illustrate this, I have lovingly referred to the area around the aura as "sacred real estate," helping to teach the significance of understanding how to expand and contract the auric field appropriately. This practice allows Indigos and other sensitives to maintain their emotional balance and safeguard their energetic space.

The very real danger of not learning the skills necessary to protect the aura can lead to a range of emotional and mental health challenges for empaths. Without effective boundaries, empathy is highly susceptible to absorbing the energy and emotions of those around them. This can result in feelings of overwhelming stress, confusion, and an inability to distinguish between their own emotions and the emotions of others. As a result, they may experience heightened levels of anxiety, depression, and even a sense of chaos in their inner world. The inability to safeguard their energetic space can lead to emotional exhaustion, leaving them feeling drained and disconnected from their true selves. Developing strong protective techniques is essential for empaths to maintain emotional balance and well-being in an often overwhelming and energy-rich environment.

Princess Diana (1961–1997) was an Indigo known for her sensitivity and kindness. Diana's compassion and genuine care for others were evident in her work with various charities, her support for the disadvantaged, and her involvement in humanitarian causes. Her ability to connect deeply with people from all social classes reflects the empathetic nature associated with Indigos.

Indigos are known for their powerful sense of individuality, a desire to challenge the status quo, and a willingness to speak up for what they believe is right. Diana consistently spoke out about issues that were often considered taboo or sensitive at the time, such as mental health, AIDS awareness, and the challenges faced by the marginalized. Her willingness to address difficult subjects demonstrated a boldness that is typical of Indigos.

Indigos are often deeply authentic and true to themselves, which can sometimes come across as outspoken or even rebellious. Diana's honesty and refusal to conform to traditional royal expectations made her stand out, allowing her to connect with people on a more personal and meaningful level.

Connection to Sensitive and Gifted Children

Michael, the Indigo introduced earlier, shares this story with us. "My wife, Dora and I left Tucson, Arizona, intending to travel to Oregon, near Mount Shasta. However, we found ourselves in Klamath Falls, where we met a young eight-year-old girl named Danni.

One morning, as we were enjoying the day, Danni joined us. Curious about her, I asked, "Danni, tell us about yourself." She looked at me with unwavering confidence and said, '*My name is Danni. I am a warrior princess. I am here to save the animals and help this world. And I will never be a doormat for anyone.*'"

Michael, this gifted Starseed, deeply connected with Indigo, stood with Danni, unwavering in her mission on this Earth.

Michael continues sharing his experience, "One day, Danni and I were walking through a forest of towering pine trees, stepping into an open meadow. As I glanced to my left, I noticed a flawless line of large birds soaring across the sky. "Danni, look over there," I said, pointing at the formation. She squinted, then shook her head. *'I can't see that, Michael,'* she responded. Then, with a gesture straight ahead, she asked, *'But what about over there?'* I followed her gaze, and what happened next still leaves me in awe.

Two large, white pelicans emerged from the pines, soaring upward. She pointed again. *'What about there?'* Turning around, I watched two more pelicans lift gracefully from the trees behind us, ascending into the sky. She pointed to my left. *'And there?'* Again, two more birds rose, their wings stretching toward the heavens. *'And what about there?'* she asked, gesturing to my right. Two more took flight, side by side, flapping their wings in unison as they climbed higher. I stood mesmerized, watching them rise. Then, as I looked up, I saw something extraordinary. The birds had tucked their wings in and were now gliding effortlessly in the sky, tracing the shape of an infinity symbol, no more than thirty feet above us."

Michael understands that he was able to share this extraordinary experience with this gifted child because of her high vibrational frequency, one that the pelicans recognized and sought to honor.

Michael concludes his interview with these reflections, "My wife, Dora, and I traveled across the country, searching for kindred spirits and spiritual communities. And do you know what? We found them in the preschool classroom. These children have clear minds and function beautifully, brilliantly. That is why it must start at the preschool level. These children come in unburdened, with completely open hearts and minds.

This is the time to help them discover their true selves, to gift them an understanding of who they are. That way, when they enter the educational system, it will not overwhelm them. This is why we created the Sacred Selves Learning Program."

In closing this chapter, let us take a moment to honor the mission of the Indigo souls who have played a crucial role in dismantling outdated beliefs and helping humanity shift from division to diversity. They have broken barriers and paved the way for the necessary changes on our planet to facilitate the birth of the New Earth.

Indigos continue their mission by guiding, awakening, and holding energetic space for the other rays that incarnated after them. I would like to sincerely thank Michael for sharing his stories with us in such an eloquent manner. Michael and his wife Dora are clients whom I will always hold deep in my heart, as the sessions conducted with them were deeply impactful and significantly influenced the trajectory of all our lives. And thank you to Sally Rice, who truly embodies the Indigo Ray.

We extend our deepest gratitude to our Indigo Starseeds, courageous pioneers who introduced transformative new paradigms, laying the groundwork for the Blue Ray, Crystal, Rainbow, Diamond Ray, Golden Ray, and Solar Ray Children who continue their work.

Chapter 3

Blue Rays and the Transmutation of Energy

Blue Ray Starseeds began incarnating on our planet in the 1960s and continue to do so today. Their mission was divinely orchestrated as part of a larger strategy to integrate the Blue Ray energy signature into the Earth's energetic field. Various Starseeds answered the call, arriving at distinct stages along the journey of ascension to fulfill this purpose.

The earliest wave of Blue Rays made a soul-level agreement to hold and stabilize this frequency, creating a foundation for future Blue Ray incarnations. Their role was to anchor and amplify the energy, making it more accessible to those who would follow in subsequent decades.

The best way to describe the essence of a Blue Ray being is that they arrive through the Blue Ray itself, a vibrational frequency of the eighth ray, integrated by the color blue. These Starseeds originate from multiple planets, stars, and galaxies, carrying the distinct resonance of the Blue Ray wherever they incarnate. Blue Ray Starseeds can incarnate from the 6th, 7th, 8th, or 9th dimensions, depending on their soul origins and mission.

Currently, most Blue Ray Starseeds on Earth hold frequencies that originate primarily from Sirius B, Orion, Pleiades, Andromeda, and Arcturus.

However, Blue Rays also come from numerous other cosmic locations, each bringing their own unique energetic imprint to assist in Earth's ascension.

Sacred Polarity: Uniting the Missions of the Indigo and Blue Ray Souls

Blue Ray Starseeds began incarnating around the same time as the Indigos, each carrying distinct yet complementary energetic signatures. While Indigos vibrate at the purple/indigo frequency of the third eye chakra, Blue Rays resonate with the blue ray, deeply connected to the throat chakra and the power of expression.

Though they incarnated within the same period, these two soul groups agreed on a higher level to embody vastly different polarities within the energetic spectrum. This contrast was intentional and designed to create a powerful dynamic energetic shift on the planet. Both groups understand the spiritual law of polarity, knowing that by holding opposite yet harmonious frequencies, they would catalyze a faster and more profound transformation in humanity's awakening.

Indigos come to confront, challenge, and disrupt, but in a transformative, powerful way. Indigos are the ones who stand up and say, *no, this is not right.* They question everything and refuse to accept what does not make sense, and at times are thrown out of churches and schools. There is an inherent boldness, an unwavering determination to seek truth, no matter the cost. From the Blue Ray perspective, it is about a deeper level of activation.

Moreover, a distinctive feature of Blue Ray individuals is their ability to embody the clarity of the soul blueprint, guiding others in anchoring energy, awakening their innate healing powers, and transforming stagnant or dense energies into lighter, more vibrant states. Their presence serves as a guiding force in helping humanity navigate the ascension process with clarity, balance, and authenticity.

Meredith, a Blue Ray born June 13, 1984, elaborates on why she never resonated with being an Indigo, "I am not an activist, not a protester, not someone who is in your face. I have always been more of a behind-the-scenes kind of person.

I guess, in a way, I see myself as a sort of *ethnic model UN*, but for the Galactic's. I do not really belong to just one lineage, which is a big indicator of being a Blue Ray. They do not originate from just one place, and neither do I. I am more of a wanderer, a Starseed that moves between different realms, various times. At some point, whether through meditation or just an intuitive download, I came to understand that one of the reasons I incarnate on Earth is to be here during times of transformation, to help facilitate vibrational shifts in some way. It is not about being on the frontlines; it is about working in the background, holding space for change."

Meredith continues, "I feel deeply connected to past lifetimes in Lemuria, Atlantis, and ancient Egypt. There is something about Hathor and about Hatshepsut that resonates with me. I remember in a channeling class, I started seeing this planet of cats, and suddenly, that vision shifted into Sekhmet, into Hatshepsut, into this ancient Egyptian reverence for feline energy. And somehow, it all connected back to the Hathors to energy work, to sound healing.

That is the thing about being a Blue Ray, many times, we work from behind the curtain. For the longest time, I did not think I did planetary healing or grid work. But sometimes, the things we believe we *are not* doing are the things we have been doing all along."

Blue Ray Gateway to Higher Realms

Julie Kraus, a Blue Ray and professional Psychic Medium, was born on June 18, 1984. "I deeply resonate with the term *Starseed* because of my strong connection to extraterrestrials and channeling them. I regularly connect with the Sirius Collective, Pleiadeans, Arcturians, and other beings.

As a child, primarily under 10 years old. I experienced frequent abductions, though I did not fully understand them at the time. Every night, I felt an otherworldly presence watching me. I would wake up half-dressed, with nosebleeds, hanging off my bed, or in different parts of the house—sometimes even sleepwalking without triggering alarms my parents had set up.

I also recall seeing a beam of light in my backyard with a being standing beneath it.

Now, as I effortlessly channel Galactic beings, my cosmic brothers and sisters, I know these experiences shaped me. I have even been told I have hybrid children who visit the Redwoods in California. These encounters, spanning from early childhood into my teens, have happened countless times, leaving me with a deep, undeniable knowing."

Meredith explains her connection to the galactic realm, "It was sometime around 2019, when I had this experience. I remember waking up in the middle of the night and seeing four or five small beings lined up at the foot of my bed. They were not threatening, I could tell that much, but they had draped themselves in these long, flowing robes, like ancient druids you would see in movies. Except they were short, like Ewoks from *Star Wars*, but in those robes.

I had a deep knowing that they were Arcturians. And this was not the only time I encountered them. On another night, I woke up to the feeling of someone touching my arm. As I stirred, I heard a voice say, "*She's not ready yet.*" The moment I fully woke up, the Arcturian figure standing by me just faded away.

The most distinct thing about them was the shape of their heads. It is hard to describe—like a trapezoid inside a square, inside a circle. Very geometric, very otherworldly.

The whole experience felt like they were checking in on me, like they were visiting to see if I recognized them yet. It was as if I knew them, not like *me* in this life, in this body, but from another lifetime or dimension. It felt like they were waiting to see if I was ready to start collaborating with them, to receive the knowledge they had. Like they were not just here to *teach* me something, but to *help me remember*—like the wisdom was already there, buried inside me, just waiting to be unlocked."

Harmonic Messengers: Knowing the Mission, Remembering the Origin

Another defining trait of Blue Ray Starseeds is their innate awareness of their mission, many times from an early age. They carry a deep, unshakable understanding that they are not from this world, often feeling a sense of disconnection from human society and its structures. This awareness can create feelings of isolation, as they intuitively recognize their origins beyond Earth.

Natalie Viglione, founder of *Awakening Magick*, explains her emergence to the Blue Ray Energy, "In early 2020, I found myself in a state of transition, feeling an undeniable pull toward something greater. One day, while meditating alone on a greenway near my home, I was in deep contemplation, searching for an answer just beyond my reach.

Then, in an instant, everything changed. A force hit me on the back of my head, slamming me to the ground. As I lay there, overwhelmed, a vision unfolded before me. On my left shoulder stood a line of women, an unbroken ancestral lineage stretching beyond time. Tears streamed down my face, though I could not yet grasp why.

When I sat up, a flood of memories surged through me. Vivid shades of turquoise and deep azure filled my mind's eye, accompanied by an intense series of activations, each revelation striking in rapid succession. Over time, as I integrated the experience, I realized I had tapped into something ancient, the universal mother, the cosmic mother.

As the pieces fell into place, I understood, I was connecting to the mother of Dragons lineage, and ultimately, my own avatar self. Every aspect of my soul's existence collapsed into oneness, marking the moment of my full awakening as a Blue Ray Soul Starseed."

Natalie continues as she describes the dragon layer, "In the summer of 2023, I began receiving powerful transmissions from the mother of Dragons. It was relentless, as the visions, dreams, and messages poured through me. I wrote feverishly, trying to keep up with what felt like an ancient remembering awakening within me. The crop circles called me, encouraging me to decode their symbols. They all pointed to one place: Avebury, October 2023.

As fate would have it, a friend casually mentioned a trip to Glastonbury. The timing was terrible as I was in the middle of moving, but there was no question. I had to go.

On October 27, 2023, I visited Avebury Henge. That day, I absorbed a dragon egg into my field, a moment so profound, so undeniable, that I documented it all in photographs. This was not just a personal activation; it was part of something greater.

This awakening is about restoring balance, the true dragon consciousness re-emerging to heal the land, to unite the divine masculine and feminine, first within the earth, and then within us. Or, both at once."

Blue Rays and Seeing the Divine Potential Within Others

Another high-vibrational characteristic of Blue Ray Starseeds is their ability to see and recognize the highest potential in others.

While some Starseeds incarnate to work through the shadow aspect of judgment, most Blue Rays are naturally gifted with the ability to peer beyond the surface, seeing deep into the window of the soul and reading the energy of the heart chakra. This allows them to discern a pure heart and understand a person's true essence and potential beyond any external limitations.

Because of this unique ability, Blue Rays excel as guides, mentors, and transformational healers. They are naturally suited for roles such as Life and Soul Coaches, where they assist others in dissolving energetic blockages, shedding layers of limitation, and stepping fully into their divine purpose. Their compassion, intuitive insight, and energetic sensitivity make them powerful catalysts for healing and personal evolution, helping individuals align with their highest timeline and soul mission.

Julie explains, "As an old soul, I feel deeply called not only to offer readings but also to teach and guide others on their spiritual journey. Through my firsthand experiences, I have navigated profound challenges that have taught me the depths of compassion and unconditional love, for myself and for others. These lessons have given me the ability to understand those I connect with, whether I am guiding them through their struggles or teaching them to embrace their own gifts. My journey has shaped me so that when I help others, I do so with a knowing that comes from the core of my being."

Clearing Ancestral Karma and Transmuting Energies

The energetic signature of the Blue Rays is one of profound healing, deeply intertwined with their soul blueprint and mission. Their purpose includes clearing ancestral karma, holding space, and anchoring high-frequency energy to assist others in healing and transmuting dense energies. This work is essential in dissolving energetic blockages or cycles of unresolved trauma, false narratives, and lower vibrational imprints that keep both individuals and the collective in a repetitive loop of limitation.

Currently, the Blue Rays have a collective mission to assist humanity in clearing stagnant energy, creating a powerful vibrational shift that elevates the frequency of the collective consciousness. A unique aspect of the Blue Ray Starseeds is that they have incarnated over decades, strategically arriving at different points in Earth's timeline to support the planet's ascension process.

Meredith describes one of the missions of a Blue Ray Starseed, "Blue Rays have a mission to hold energetic space for all the changes happening on Earth. That is part of our role, to anchor and stabilize energy during these times of transformation. For me, my awakening really began through Reiki. Of course, this has always been who I am, but for a long time, I shut it down. Through past life regressions, I have seen that even in my mother's womb, I was already healing her energy, transmuting negativity before I was even born. And once I entered this world, that pattern continued. I became the one in the family who absorbed everyone's energy, trying to bring harmony."

Meredith explains, "I always felt this deep need for justice, for fairness, for balance. Of course, that meant I had a rough childhood. I was always the one trying to make things better, trying to ease the burdens of those around me. Then, I had a Reiki healing session that changed everything. I remember looking at the woman working on me, and in that moment, some of my energy transferred onto her. I saw my own face reflected in hers, but aged, like I was looking at myself 30 years into the future. That is when it clicked: *I can learn Reiki.*

So, I studied Reiki, eventually becoming a Reiki Master Teacher, and that is when my intuitive gifts really started coming into focus. But honestly, I did not fully recognize them for what they were, *not really*, until I met Jill and completed her training in psychic development and mediumship development."

Natalie describes part of her mission, "The Blue Ray is about transmutation, transforming the darkest, most vile energies, the ones that most spiritual lightworkers shy away from. One of the strongest aspects of the Blue Ray revealed itself when I began to *feel* Gaia, not just connecting with her, but embodying her pain. If someone sprayed pesticides or poured poison into the earth, I did not just witness it, I *felt* it, as if it were happening to me. The connection was so intense that I would collapse, overcome by grief, melting into the ground as if I were part of it."

She continues, "This awakening ignited deeper layers within me. My work, my purpose, became clearer, I was not just here to transmute energy for the earth, but also for individuals. Through vibrational medicine, I began to see lineages, soul patterns, things I had never accessed before. The Blue Ray activated something latent within me, enabling me to assist others in their personal development, mirroring the guidance I had received during my own transformation."

Aligned with Archangel Michael and Celestial Blue Beings

Quite a few people who resonate with and embody the Blue Ray frequency share a deep connection with Archangel Michael, as well as with higher-dimensional beings who naturally embody the blue ray of light. These Starseeds often have an innate ability to perceive and communicate with these celestial blue beings, a connection that has been present within them for as long as they can remember. This bond serves as a guiding force, offering wisdom, protection, and activation throughout their soul's journey.

Although I connect deeply with Indigo energy, I also carry the Blue Ray frequency in my aura.

For example, I have had the absolute pleasure of seeing Archangel Michael. He appeared just as He has always been described, very tall and radiant, glowing with divine light.

It happened while I was driving out of Angel Valley, Sedona, at the end of a powerful 7-day Past Life Regression course. That land ... that retreat ... it was truly magical in more ways than I can count. None of us wanted to leave.

My Reiki Master teacher, Joan, was in the car with me. We were still on the sacred land, winding around a curve in the road when suddenly we stopped in front of a large mountain.

And there, standing tall at the very top of it, was Archangel Michael.

I stopped the car, and my jaw completely dropped. I glanced over at Joan, and she was doing the exact same thing. I asked her, "Are you seeing what I'm seeing?" And without taking her eyes off Him, she said, "Yes. It is Archangel Michael."

We just sat there, frozen in awe, tears streaming down our cheeks, staring at this pure, divine form.

I will never forget that moment. It was one of the most profound and sacred experiences of my life.

But the magic—and the synchronicity—did not stop there.

Years later, while leading my own retreat at Angel Valley, the administrator was walking me through the map of the land. She was so excited to show me the mountains surrounding this sacred valley, explaining how each one was named after an archangel.

Imagine my surprise and delight when I saw the name of the mountain that sits around the curve as you drive out of the valley, the very same place where I had seen Archangel Michael.

You guessed it: Michael's Mountain.

When I asked her why that mountain was named after Archangel Michael, she simply smiled and said, *"There have been countless sightings of him on that mountain."*

Meredith discussed her deep connection to Andromeda, "In a channeling class with Jill, where we met our galactic guides, I had this incredible experience. I remember connecting with this being who felt so strongly tied to Andromeda. She had this blue skin and a distinct cone-shaped head, and something about her presence just radiated familiarity. I knew, deep down, that she was my galactic mother.

On a soul level, she had been with me through lifetimes, guiding me, loving me. And in that moment, the connection I felt with her, the unconditional love, was so profound that it almost felt stronger than what I had known in this lifetime with my own mother. Just thinking about it now makes me emotional because it was such a pure, overwhelming love.

We did not communicate with words; it was all telepathic. But there was this instant recognition, this immediate comfort. I just wanted to stay with her, to exist in that space with her presence surrounding me.

And in a way, I feel like that was her gift to me, reminding me what true, unconditional love is. Just being in that energy was healing. It was like she was showing me, through her presence alone, the essence of love in its purest form."

Natalie recalls the Blue Ray energy has always been around her, "The Blue Ray presence was always there since childhood, lingering, the apparition in the corners of my room. I could sense it, like a distant whisper, but it was something I had to journey toward, a path I had yet to walk. Looking back, I saw the signs were always there. I even authored a poem as a child called *The Blueberry Corner.* I was in sixth grade at the time, and though I didn't fully understand it then, I can now recognize it for what it was, a glimpse of the Blue Ray calling to me, waiting for the moment I was ready to step into it."

Where Light Meets Darkness, Truth Emerges

Another key mission of the Blue Rays is to hold and anchor a vibrational resonance that naturally illuminates corruption, falsehoods, and the energetic control structures of the false matrix that have shaped your planet. Their frequency acts as a catalyst, gently yet powerfully revealing hidden truths and dissolving outdated dogmas.

Blue Ray Starseeds carry a unique energetic signature that supports the unveiling of truth, making this one of their primary soul missions. Through their presence and higher awareness, they assist in shifting collective consciousness toward authenticity, sovereignty, and divine clarity.

This is another character trait I recognize in myself. I have a fearless drive to bring truth, expose fraud, and use my voice to empower. Speaking out against injustice has sometimes rattled cages, but challenging limiting beliefs rooted in deceit is part of my mission.

Natalie reflects, "Back in 2020, I launched a site called *Rise Up in Truth.* It was my space to document everything I had come to understand since my mid-twenties, the deeper truths about the world, from Big Pharma to hidden systems of control. I merged the site into *Awakening Magick,* maintaining its purpose: to illuminate darkness and spotlight the truth.

That is the nature of the Blue Ray, bringing hidden knowledge to the surface, exposing corruption, and activating truth. Now, as I bring my first poetry book into the world, *The Reclamation of All That is Organic and Pure Harmony Through the Blue Ray of Creation,* I feel that same energy flowing through it. A beautifully designed collection, something to sit with, to absorb. It is all part of the unfolding, one revelation, one creation at a time."

Aligning Voice and Frequency Through the Throat Chakra

Another key vibrational signature of the Blue Rays is their enhanced connection to the throat chakra, granting them a profound ability to work with the power of voice and frequency. Currently, on our planet, they play a crucial role in assisting others in speaking their authentic truth while also clearing energies that no longer resonate with divine alignment.

Blue Ray Starseeds have natural healing abilities, and their voices can be used for sound healing, toning, and music to shift vibrational frequencies in individuals and the Earth. Additionally, Blue Rays have a unique capacity to speak in Light Language, a form of vibrational communication that transmits healing frequencies directly through the throat chakra, facilitating deep transformation on a multidimensional level.

Many Blue Rays have the purpose of using their voice to teach others. Considering that Blue Rays were among the initial pioneers along with the Indigos, it is logical that they undertook a mission to impart their knowledge to Starseeds who have been incarnating in recent years.

Julie uses her voice for teaching, "On Instagram, I create short reels called *Magic Class,* where I teach my kids about their aura, how to stay centered, meditate, and connect with their energy. Every Thursday, we have *Magic Class*, and I share these moments because so many people are seeking ways to support their own children emotionally and intuitively."

Meredith marvels at how she has always connected to blue. "I have so many planets in Mercury, and now that I think about it, my life is *covered* in blue. If you looked in my closet, you would see so many blue clothes. My bedroom? My bedspread is blue. I am just now realizing how much blue surrounds me, like I subconsciously surround myself with that energy. And of course, blue connects to the throat chakra.

If my throat chakra is blocked, it is unbearable. I will implode, completely shut down. I have come to understand that my words carry great power. I can either be incredibly sharp and cutting, or I can be soothing, harmonizing. I must be mindful of how I use that energy because I *feel* its impact."

She continues, "After learning more about the Blue Ray, especially the healing work they do, I have begun connecting the dots. My body always *hurts*. I am constantly experiencing things that are not mine, emotions, physical sensations, energy that I know I have absorbed from others. And I have realized that healing is not something with which I will ever be done. It is ongoing. I do ancestral healing. I feel like I am working through deep feminine healing, too. It is like there is always something moving through me, something being transmuted."

Blue Ray's Connection with Oceanic Animals and Beings

Some Blue Ray Starseeds share a profound connection with the higher vibrational beings of the oceans, particularly whales and dolphins. These magnificent mammals are advanced sentient beings who carry vast amounts of cosmic wisdom, light codes, and ancient Earth knowledge.

Blue Rays often feel an innate bond with these oceanic beings, sensing their role as guardians of planetary frequency. Many Blue Rays have the natural ability to communicate telepathically with whales and dolphins, receiving light-coded transmissions that assist in their own awakening and mission work.

This connection extends beyond Earth, as whales and dolphins have interdimensional origins, with strong ties to Sirius B, the Pleiades, and Arcturus. The songs and frequencies emitted by these oceanic beings resonate at a high vibrational level, assisting in planetary healing, frequency attunements, and the recalibration of Earth's energy grids.

Blue Ray Starseeds who resonate with this connection may feel called to work with water consciousness, sound healing, or marine conservation, recognizing that the oceans themselves hold keys to planetary ascension. Their ability to tune into the frequencies of these beings enhances their capacity for energy work, emotional healing, and vibrational realignment, both for themselves and for the collective.

Julie smiles, "It is funny, until about fifth or sixth grade, I wanted to be a marine biologist. I have always felt an incredibly deep connection to dolphins and whales, with an innate knowing that they are linked to the galactic realms."

Embracing Harmony, Balance, and Empathy

Blue Rays are also extremely sensitive beings, both emotionally and energetically. To maintain balance, they must learn to work with the energy of Mother Earth and the natural world to transmute and integrate the high-frequency vibrations they carry within their physical bodies. Connecting with nature serves as a grounding force, allowing them to stabilize their energy and fully embody their mission on this planet.

Meredith reflects, "I have always felt like I never quite fit in anywhere. At the same time, I felt both different and like I could blend in effortlessly. No matter where I have lived, I have always had multiple groups of friends, each one completely different from the other. I could move between them seamlessly, be friends with everyone, but if you put them all in the same room, they would be wondering, *who are all these eccentric people that Meredith has collected?*

I have realized my role has been to harmonize. It felt like my responsibility to bring balance to the energy around me, to smooth things out in a way that felt natural. And that is such a Blue Ray trait.

For the longest time, I thought I was just doing it with words, choosing the right ones, knowing how to navigate conversations. But now I understand that it was not just *what* I was saying, it was the energy behind it. I was influencing situations energetically, shifting things just by being present, by knowing how to steer the moment into something better.

For me, feeling validated and understood has always been important, just knowing that even if I am not the one out front, loudly standing up for a cause or making my presence known, I *am* still working my magic in the background. Most of the time, no one even sees the work I do, at times not even me.

So, if someone else is feeling this way, my advice would be to *honor* their role. Not everyone is meant to stand in the spotlight, but that does not diminish the power of their purpose. Some of us are here to transmute energy quietly, behind the scenes, and that work is just as important."

As we conclude our exploration of the Blue Ray Starseeds, let us take a moment to honor the sacred mission of these Wayshowers. By embracing the wisdom and traits of the Blue Ray, you may have experienced an awakening within yourself, recognizing a deeper connection to this lineage.

Whether you identify as a Blue Ray or simply appreciate learning about their unique qualities, I invite you to join me in expressing gratitude to all Blue Rays. A heartfelt thank you to Reiki Master Teacher Meredith, Psychic Medium Julie Kraus, and Natalie Viglione of Awakening Magick for courageously sharing their personal and profound events. Their encounters and personality traits strongly aligned with the information I had channeled about the Blue Rays' mission, validating the connection between trance channeled wisdom and real-life experiences.

Chapter 4

Crystal Children: Heart of the Cosmos

In alignment with the spiritual law of polarity, a wave of souls volunteered to incarnate, bringing balance to the bold, warrior-like energy of the Indigo Ray Starseeds. They also served as a bridge to connect the alchemical energy of the Blue Ray Starseeds. Enter the Crystal Children, arriving on the 9th Ray of Consciousness, embodying a gentle, harmonious presence that perfectly counterbalances the intensity of their Indigo and Blue Ray predecessors.

The Crystal Ray children arrived with quartz-like crystalline energy that amplifies, magnifies, and reflects. Their mission is to bring light to the world, casting illumination on what was previously hidden and forgotten. Through the crystalline frequency of the Crystal Ray, ancient wisdom that has been buried for lifetimes begins to rise again, gently awakening a deep soul remembrance within the collective. It is the divine truth that has always been there, just on the other side of the veil, waiting for us to remember.

Many who arrived on the Crystal Ray have journeyed through countless lifetimes within the Pleiadian realms. They carry within their essence a rare fusion, an innate purity of heart intertwined with the high-frequency signature of elevated consciousness.

Their soul mission was to begin the dissolution of the outer layers of the matrix, creating cracks within the illusion. Where the Indigo Ray's came to disturb and disrupt the very foundations, and the Blue Ray's began the alchemical shift of those core structures, the Crystal Ray's arrived and their presence signaled the next phase in the great unraveling, a gentle, yet potent disruption of the matrix's outermost architecture.

The most fitting way to understand this is through the metaphor of layers, each ray entering the Earth plane with a distinct role in the unraveling of illusion. Those who came in on the ninth Ray, the Ray of dissolution, carried with them an energy designed to further fracture the codes of concealed knowledge. They came to break apart the unseen energetic framework of the matrix, the one that keeps humanity stuck under an invisible glass ceiling, dimming our awareness and holding back our ascension. The Crystal Rays gently yet powerfully crack open the barriers to truth.

If we imagine the awakening process as planting a sacred tree, each soul ray plays a divine role in unfolding. It becomes a living metaphor of celestial orchestration.

The Indigo Ray came first, to break through the hardened soil, tilling the earth and preparing the ground for deep transformation.

Then came the Blue Ray, carrying the frequency of transmutation. Their role was to cleanse and purify the soil itself, to infuse it with light, and shift its essence so something new could take root.

Then came the Crystal Ray, here on a mission to plant the seeds, seeds encoded with the ancient wisdom of humanity's original divine blueprint, still resting quietly within the strands of our DNA.

These crystalline seeds hold codes of remembrance, designed to gently awaken what has been forgotten throughout lifetimes.

This part of the unfolding is for those whose consciousness has opened enough to feel and recognize the frequency of truth that the Crystal Rays now carry forward.

Their auras radiate with the clarity of a pure quartz crystal, reflecting their high-frequency, serene essence. Let us now explore the multifaceted traits of the Crystal Children, who primarily incarnated between 1990 and 2010, carrying the blueprint for love, healing, and harmony. Their divine mission continues the work of the Indigos and Blue Rays by transforming old structures with gentle wisdom and divine light.

Vision Through the Realms

Those who incarnated on the Crystal Ray possess an extraordinary ability to bridge the veils between earth and our loved ones who have transitioned to heavenly realms. *Crossing Over with John Edward* (1999–2004) was a groundbreaking television show that highlighted John Edward's remarkable mediumship abilities while helping to increase public awareness and understanding of mediumship and the concept of connecting with the spirit world. Around the same time, *The Oprah Winfrey Show* began featuring more spiritual guests on her award-winning talk show, further broadening the conversation.

Books by well-known mediums such as James Van Praagh (*Talking to Heaven*,1997) and Sylvia Browne (*The Other Side and Back*, 1999) became bestsellers, fueling a growing fascination with the gift of mediumship. This surge in interest coincided with the energetic influence of the Crystal Children, who began incarnating around 1990 and helped amplify the collective curiosity and openness toward spiritual topics.

Meg Schwarzrock, Energetic Frequency Coach and Mom to a Crystal Son, Atley, born May 18, 2009, talks about her son seeing Spirits. "Atley started figuring things out when he was about two and a half. He used to tell me there was a man in the playroom, and every time he would go in there, he would shut the door like he was locking the man inside. We just assumed it was one of his great-granddads. I did not think much of it.

Then one morning, when he was a little older, three, three and a half, we were getting ready for preschool when he suddenly said, "There's a man on your bed." I paused for a second and asked, "Oh yeah? Where is he?" Atley pointed right to a spot on the bed and said, "He's poking." It took me a moment to realize what he meant, "poking" was his way of saying smoking. And right then, it clicked. I knew exactly who it was. My granddad, John, used to smoke.

So, staying calm, I said, "Alright, well, tell him we're going to preschool, and we'll see him when we get back." Atley turned toward the bed and said, "Okay, bye! We are going to preschool. See you when we get back!" And just like that, he went on with his day, like seeing spirits was the most normal thing in the world."

Another mother to a Crystal daughter named Brooklyn, born August 25, 1997, also shares her perspectives. Kerrilynn Shellhorn, Psychic Medium, says, "She has always been very in tune with the other side. Her first conscious memory of seeing someone is her father's father."

Healing Through Past Life Awareness

Crystal Ray Children are born with dormant spiritual codes embedded within their DNA, keys to ancient wisdom and soul experiences accumulated over many lifetimes. At various junctures throughout their lives, these codes activate, unlocking vivid memories and emotional imprints from their past lives. These past life remembrances often come with an intuitive understanding of sacred knowledge, healing techniques, or spiritual truths that seem far beyond their current age.

By tapping into these soul memories, Crystal Ray Children can navigate their present lifetime with a sense of purpose and inner knowing, offering healing, guidance, and light to those around them. Their connection to whom they have been not only enriches their own path but also acts as a beacon for collective healing and spiritual evolution.

Meg shares her journey of helping her son Atley navigate and release emotions that were never his to carry. "At first, it was just stomachaches. Little complaints here and there. But by the time Atley was in kindergarten, I had to walk him into school every single morning. By third grade, nothing had changed. I was still walking him in, and the nurse was still calling me almost daily. 'Atley's in the office, his stomach hurts.' It went on like this for years. Sometimes, the cafeteria was too much for him, the noise, the energy, so he would sit at a separate table with a teacher, where it was quiet.

At the time, I was not thinking about energy or anything spiritual. I grew up in a medical household, so my first thought was, *what is wrong with my child?* That summer, right before fourth grade, things got worse. He started throwing up after almost every meal. His eyes had deep, dark circles under them, and soon, he began associating food with sickness, he did not want to eat at all.

While he was struggling with all of this, I tried to get to the root of it. I would ask, 'Is there anyone making you feel uncomfortable? Is something going on?' And that is when he started telling me things. 'My teacher is really sad. Her daughter just went to college.' Or, 'She is upset. She is going through something.' He was absorbing emotions that were never his to carry. And that is when I started to wonder, was his stomach pain, even his at all?

Then, one day, while I was taking a class on energy healing, Atley walked into my room, went straight to the balcony, and threw up. Right after, a woman from the class called me. 'Do you realize how much pain he is in?' she said. My stomach feels distended, full of gas pains. This is not about food. This is energetic.

She connected me with an energy healer the very next day. The healer asked if she could talk to Atley about past lives. "Can I have these conversations with a fourth grader? she asked. I told her, 'Absolutely. We have these conversations in our house.'

And so, the real work began. She helped clear past-life trauma, and we adjusted his diet to slowly heal his system so he could reintegrate the foods he loved. By September, just a couple of months later, Atley was eating again. He was not throwing up after every meal.

The healer told me something that stuck with me: 'Meg, he is absorbing other people's emotions, he is internalizing their anxiety and pain, and it is manifesting physically in his body. But it is not his.'"

Meg continues, "That moment shifted everything for me. I thought about how, in the medical world, we go straight to diagnoses, treatments, medications. But what if the root of the problem isn't physical? What if it is spiritual? If we had kept going on the traditional medical route, I have no doubt he would have been diagnosed with an autoimmune disorder, placed on lifelong infusions, labeled with an illness that was not even truly his. Instead, he learned how to transmute it, to understand his sensitivity, rather than suffer because of it."

Mission to Collaborate with the Spirit World

Many individuals who incarnated on the Crystal Ray came into this lifetime with a soul purpose of working with those residing in the astral or in-between realms. They naturally possess a deep understanding of subtle energy signatures and an innate ability to hold space with a loving, pure heart. This unique combination allows them to compassionately assist others by navigating these realms with grace and clarity.

Meg remembers this amazing experience with her son Atley. "It was sometime around October when Atley stepped onto the porch, eyes wide with surprise. 'A man just walked through the living room,' he said. I froze for a moment. This had not happened since he was a little boy. 'Oh really?' I asked, trying to stay calm. A few moments later, he ran into my room, visibly shaking. 'That man's back! He just came through my door!' His voice was filled with panic. Whatever he had seen, it was not just a passing shadow, it was real to him.

Not wanting to dismiss his experience, I immediately called the energy healer we had been working with. As soon as she picked up, she paused, then said, 'I am feeling this is a man who recently passed. He is confused, and he knows that Atley can help him.'

Atley looked at me, completely baffled. 'Me,' he whispered. Lily, the energy healer, gently explained to him, 'Atley, you have a gift. But it is not your job to help every spirit that comes to you. You can always call on your angels to guide them to the light. Or, as you get older and learn more, you can choose to help when you feel called. But remember, it is always your choice. With her guidance, Atley helped the man cross over. From that moment on, we never saw him again."

Psychic Medium Kerrilynn Shellhorn is also Mom to a Crystal son Ryan born October 20, 1994. Kerrilynn describes Ryan as a deep thinker who tends to be more reserved about his experiences. "There were the night terrors, constant, intense, and relentless. When he was two and three, he experienced them all the time. It was heartbreaking to watch, and at the time, I did not fully understand what was happening.

Now, looking back, I realize he was slipping into dimensional spaces he was not meant to linger in, realms beyond his years, beyond what he was ready to navigate."

She continues, "Around the age of 12 or 13, he started having profound encounters that felt distinctly otherworldly. He would wake me up in the middle of the night, describing how he had been floating or astral traveling. He would say, 'I was moving really fast, and there were lights all around me.' He vividly recalled floating down the hallway, watching over us as we slept—fully aware and conscious of the experience."

Natural Energetic Healer

One of the most defining traits of a Crystal Ray Starseed is their innate ability to channel energy and support others in healing both physical and emotional wounds. Many are naturally drawn to energy-based healing modalities such as Reiki, Esoteric Healing, Quantum Healing, Chios Healing, and others. Often, they carry a deep inner knowing, a soul memory of lifetimes spent practicing these arts. In some cases, they begin intuitively running energy through their palms even before formal training, with classes simply serving to refine and awaken an already present spiritual gift.

Looking back on this moment, Meg feels an overwhelming sense of pride in her son, knowing how deeply compassionate and intuitive he is. "It was Christmas, and our house was full of family. One of those chilly holiday afternoons where everyone is hanging around, unsure of what to do. So, I made the call, *we are all going bowling.*

We got to the alley, settled into our lanes, and started having fun. Everything was fine until Atley suddenly clutched his stomach. His face shifted, that all-too-familiar discomfort settling in.

By then, thanks to working with Lily, the energy healer, Atley had learned to ask himself an important question: *Is what I am feeling mine, or is it someone else's?*

He took a deep breath. 'I need some fresh air,' he said.

I nodded and walked outside with him. 'Alright, is it yours or someone else's?' I asked gently. He hesitated for a moment, then answered, 'It is the little boy who just came in to bowl next to us. He is really sad and scared.' That caught my attention. I had noticed the boy too, quiet and withdrawn, like he was carrying something heavy.

Lily had also taught Atley to use colors to shift energy. 'What color are you being shown that could help him?' I asked. Atley closed his eyes for a moment. 'Green,' he said.

So, we stood outside, and Atley focused, sending that healing green energy toward the boy, wrapping him in it. A few moments passed. Then, Atley let out a breath and smiled. 'Okay. I feel better now.'

And just like that, we walked back inside, picked up our game, and kept bowling, like nothing had happened. But I knew something *had* happened. Atley had just helped someone, without them even knowing, simply by listening to what he felt and trusting what he knew."

Intuitive Awareness Through Clairsentience

Clairsentience is a form of extrasensory perception in which intuitive information is received primarily through feeling. Those with clairsentient abilities can sense the vibrations or energies of other people and themselves, often picking up on emotions, physical sensations, or moods without any verbal communication. Crystal Ray Starseeds possess a deep understanding of energy through their sensitivities.

Kerrilynn looks back on Ryan's psychic abilities, "By the time he reached grade nine, his first year of exams, I was already deeply immersed in my spiritual work, I had a spiritual parenting radio show and was having much more open conversations with my kids than when they were younger.

During that year, when he was around 13 or 14, he started asking deeper questions. One day, he said, Remember that thing?'

I asked, 'Which thing?'

He replied, 'The thing where we can ask people on the other side to help us.'

I smiled and said, 'Of course, I remember. What happened?'

He told me that during his science exam, he hit a mental block and could not remember what he needed to do. So, he took a deep breath and asked if Albert Einstein could come in and help him understand the question.

I told him, 'That is exactly how you ask for guidance—not for them to do the work for you, but to help you understand. So, what happened?'

He lit up and said, 'It was like fireworks! I felt grounded, and everything just flowed. I was able to finish easily.'

I asked, 'And how did that feel?'

He smiled, 'Really good.'"

Kerrilynn explains, "That was not the only time he used this practice. He continued doing it, especially when it came time for exams and music. Later, when he was accepted into a prestigious music program, like Glee, where students recorded, produced, and toured, he called me from school and said, 'Mom, remember that thing you taught me?'

I laughed, 'Which thing, Ryan?'

He said, 'The one where we take a breath, put our hand over our heart, and ask our higher self if something is right for us.'

I asked, 'What happened?'

He told me he used it to decide whether he should go to a party. He checked in with himself, asked how each option felt, and then made his choice. He regrets not following his intuition and making the wrong choice, but he learned from the experience.

He has really embraced listening to his intuition, understanding that the consequences of ignoring it can be far greater than just listening to begin with."

Kerrilynn remarks how her Crystal daughter Brooklyn has always been sensitive, "She discovered that for a significant period of her life, her intuition was loudest when it was a do not go, like a flashing red warning sign.

She would say, 'My gut told me not to do this, and it went sideways.' And after experiencing this pattern over and over, I finally said, 'Okay, now pay attention. If your gut is telling you not to do something and it keeps leading to chaos when you do it, try going the other way and see what happens.'

That shift changed everything. She started discerning between true guidance and instinctual reactions, and as she fine-tuned that awareness, she began to see just how magical life really is." Kerrilynn laughs, "But even from an early age, she would hold me accountable. She would say, 'Your energy feels off-kilter, and it's affecting everyone in the room.'

And she was not wrong."

She was incredibly tuned in, even as early as grade three, four, or five, she could sense shifts in energy before anyone else and was not afraid to call it out.

Telepathic Tendencies

Telepathy is the ability to transmit or receive thoughts, feelings, or information directly from one mind to another without the use of spoken words, physical signals, or traditional senses. It is a form of intuitive communication that transcends physical boundaries, often described as *soul-to-soul* or *heart-to-heart* transmission.

While telepathy is prominent among the Rainbow Rays, and the Rays that followed them, some Crystal Rays also showed this ability early on.

Kerrilynn remains amazed by the telepathic connection she shares with her daughter. "Among all my children, she is the one who has genuinely grasped telepathic communication, and we continue to use it to this day," she states.

"If I find myself thinking about her or missing her since she lives an hour away, she will often text me unexpectedly. Just recently, I told her, 'Honey, I was thinking about you this morning, and I ordered something for you, it should be on your doorstep this afternoon.' And she replied, 'I was literally looking at that last night!' These synchronicities happen between us all the time.

Back when she was in fourth grade, she loved practicing these abilities. I remember one time in the car, it was October, and she asked, 'If I guess what I'm getting for Christmas, will you tell me?'

I said,' Sure—but you get only one guess.'

I kept thinking *pink Nintendo DS* in my mind, and sure enough, she said, 'Oh! You got me the pink Nintendo DS!'

I just laughed and said, 'Yes, I did, babe. Yes, I did. And isn't it going to suck waiting from October to December to open it?'

That moment made me realize that if I ever wanted to keep something from her, I would have to be very mindful of my own thoughts!"

Highly Sensitive & Empathic

Crystal Rays are known for their pure hearts, gentle spirits, and radiant, loving auras that naturally draw others toward them. They exude a calming presence and often carry a deep sense of empathy and emotional intelligence from an early age. With an innate drive to serve, their life purpose is often centered around helping others, whether through healing, emotional support, creative expression, or simply being a light in the lives of those around them.

Their compassion is genuine and natural. Crystal Rays often feel a strong calling to make the world a more harmonious and peaceful place, and they do so through quiet acts of kindness, heartfelt communication, and an unwavering commitment to love in action.

Kerrilynn is incredibly proud of her Crystal daughter Brooklyn, "Now, she is on the path of academia, working toward her PhD. She studied child and youth development, completed her undergraduate, her master's, and a year into her PhD, she decided to take a break. Even in high school, she was always giving back, volunteering with people with disabilities, playing sledge hockey with them, and just being an amazing all-around human. She is a phenomenal soul and always has been."

Fascinated with Crystals

Crystals are naturally formed within the heart of Mother Earth over thousands, sometimes millions of years, shaped by intense heat, pressure, and the unique alchemy of minerals present in their environment. Each crystal carries its own distinct vibrational frequency, acting as a conduit for subtle energies. This frequency is influenced by the crystal's composition, color, geometric structure, and formation process.

Several types of crystals and stones hold specific energetic properties, some are known for grounding and protection, while others promote healing, clarity, or spiritual connection. Just as each human has a unique energetic signature, so too does each crystal, making them powerful allies in energy work, meditation, and spiritual growth.

Crystal Ray Starseeds are naturally attracted to rocks and crystals, often using them in their daily lives.

Meg reflects, "As Atley grew, so did his understanding of energy. He learned about crystals, mudras, meditation, and breathwork, tools that helped him navigate the intensity of the world around him.

One night, he had a friend sleep over. At some point, the friend glanced around and frowned. 'Why do you have rocks all over your bed?' he asked, clearly puzzled.

Atley just shrugged. 'Oh ... you wouldn't understand.'

Meg reflects on the moments when she felt lonely, isolated, and misunderstood, realizing how often she walked a path that few could truly relate to. So many parents are still trying to mold their kids to fit neatly into the box, to be just like everyone else. I never wanted that for my children, but it does come with its challenges. While Atley and his siblings might not feel lonely in their own experiences, there are times when *I* do. Sometimes, I look around and realize just how different we are from most of the world. And in those moments, it can feel isolating, like we exist on the edges of something much bigger, just trying to find where we belong."

Within Meg's raw and unfiltered expression of feeling detached and disconnected from much of the world, you might feel a reflection stir within your own soul.

It is hard to truly grasp the weight and wonder of walking the path of a pioneer, whether through your own Starseed lineage, through parenting Starseed children, or both.

My hope, and my prayer, is that those who feel called to this book will recognize a deep soul resonance with the voices shared in these chapters. And in that recognition, may you deepen your awareness of your own sacred mission.

As we conclude the Crystal Starseed chapter, you may notice a subtle shift in your own energy, feeling more relaxed, balanced, and calm. You might even recognize the unique traits of the Crystal Ray within yourself, or in your children or grandchildren.

Take a moment with me now to inhale deeply, anchoring pure heart energy into your auric field. Let us pause and offer heartfelt gratitude to those who chose to incarnate on the Crystal Ray. Their mission to heal, understand past life energies, and work in harmony with the spirit world serves as a beautiful gift to humanity. With love and reverence, we honor their contributions to the collective journey of healing and spiritual growth.

Please join me in expressing gratitude to Meg Schwarzrock, an Energetic Frequency Coach, and Kerrilynn Shellhorn, a Psychic Medium, for generously sharing inspiring stories of their remarkable Crystal Ray Children.

Chapter 5

Rainbow Children: Bridge Between Worlds

The Rainbow Children began arriving in greater numbers between 2005 and 2015. They are associated with the tenth ray of consciousness and are known for their ability to hold a wide range of energetic frequencies, often reflected in the colorful, layered quality of their aura, hence the name "Rainbow." These children naturally embody a balance between masculine and feminine energies and often bring a deep sense of harmony to the spaces they inhabit.

Their presence also mirrors broader cultural shifts, including a growing awareness and acceptance of gender diversity. It is no coincidence that the rise of the transgender rights movement has paralleled the emergence of Rainbow Children, as both reflect a collective movement toward more fluid and inclusive understandings of identity.

In this chapter, we will explore this connection further through my trance channeling transmissions, personal stories and interviews that offer a closer look into the lives and perspectives of these remarkable young people.

Sacred Balance of Masculine and Feminine Energies

One mission of the Rainbow Rays is to promote balanced living, both within individuals and in relation to the earth. These children naturally carry both masculine and feminine qualities in a way that feels integrated and whole. They are not here to take sides or choose one energy over the other, they are here to show that both are essential and meant to work together. Through their presence and way of being, they encourage us to soften rigid, more traditional gender roles, to live with both strength and compassion, and to find harmony within ourselves first. By doing so, they help teach us how to build a more balanced and unified world.

Erin Acevedo, a Crystal Starseed, who is also a professional psychic medium, says this about her Rainbow son, Jonas, born on the Lionsgate of August 8, 2009. "Jonas has always had a beautifully balanced mix of masculine and feminine energy, seamlessly fitting in wherever he goes. Even before he was born, there were signs; when I was pregnant, I was convinced he was a girl.

As he grew up, it became even more apparent. His closest friends were always girls, and he was naturally drawn to things traditionally labeled as "feminine." As a little boy, he loved rainbows and pink and delighted in painting his nails when he was about five years old. Up until around the age of 10 or 11, he did not give much thought to gender norms. He would happily shop in the girls' section without hesitation, simply choosing what he liked rather than what was expected. For him, gender was never a defining factor, it was just not something that mattered."

Kerrilynn Shellhorn, a Psychic Medium and mother to Taylor, born on July 4, 1993, shares her thoughts on her Rainbow son. "The generation of the testosterone-filled male, gets uncomfortable around him because they can't discern where he's at, but he laughs, he giggles like a girl, but he is all guy, he's very balanced male, female." She continues, "Certain people tend to be uncomfortable around him that way."

Meg Schwarzrock, Energetic Frequency Coach, smiles as she talks about her Rainbow son, Avery, born January 2, 2006. "He is so dialed in, so balanced in both his masculine and feminine energy. He is comfortable with everyone, boys and girls alike, without feeling the need to prove anything. He has this beautiful blend of strength and sensitivity, toughness, and sweetness. He's just so perfectly balanced."

Highly Sensitive and Connected to Nature

Rainbow Children have a strong, natural connection to the Earth. Being in nature helps them feel calm, centered, and more like themselves. Whether it is walking barefoot on the ground, sitting quietly under a tree, or simply noticing the sky, they feel at home in the natural world. This connection helps them stay grounded in their bodies and in the present moment. In a time when many are disconnected from the rhythms of life, Rainbow Children remind us to slow down, breathe, and reconnect with what is real and steady beneath our feet. Through them, we are gently invited to remember that the Earth itself can be one of our greatest sources of balance and healing.

Kerrilynn remembers how sensitive her son is, "Taylor spoke late, just as his language development was delayed. He was extremely sensitive to light, sound, smells, and noise, extra sensitive to all of it."

Meg, mother to Rainbow son Avery, is grateful to have had the tools to teach her son about breathing and grounding. She reflects, "When it comes to anxiety, he knows to do his breathing exercises, and I'll see him outside, barefoot, walking in the yard. It's such a beautiful thing."

Inanna Rae, Psychic Medium, fills with joy as she remembers this occasion with her Rainbow daughter Avery, "One time, we were driving down the highway after a tornado had torn through the area. Without hesitation, she made me pull over. She insisted she needed to heal the trees. So, there we were, on the side of the road, as she stood among the broken branches, doing whatever it was she felt called to do."

Master Manifestors

What is truly remarkable about the Rainbow Ray Children is how naturally they manifest. These children often hold a deep inner knowing that what they imagine can become real and it often does. Their energy is pure, their intentions are clear, and their hearts are open, which makes them powerful co-creators. They do not just wish for things; they understand how to align their energy with them. And in doing so, they remind us that manifestation is less about control and more about connection. Watching them manifest is not only inspiring, but also a glimpse of the kind of world we are all capable of building when we remember who we are.

Erin marvels at her son Jonas with his manifesting abilities. "Jonas has this incredible ability to manifest things, it's like he just speaks something into existence, and it happens."

Kerrilynn is amazed when thinking about her son's manifesting abilities, "Taylor is a powerful manifestor, that boy is pure magic. He is incredibly gifted and plays guitar effortlessly. His photography caught the eye of someone from the United Kingdom, simply from where he dropped off his film. The recognition resulted in an exhibition, and one of his photos was selected for an international tour. His work was even featured in an installation in Calgary, Alberta, Canada."

She continues, "Another time that Taylor proved his manifesting abilities was when he moved. He had no job, no home, and no connections, just a clear intention to work for a specific company. Within a year, he was not only employed there but now, they are preparing him for partnership and leadership in education. He creates his own reality, effortlessly drawing opportunities to him."

Inanna recalls how her daughter Avery can manifest anything, "I watched my daughter do this *all the time.* It became so normal; I stopped even reacting to it. We would walk into one of those kid casinos, Chuck E. Cheese, places like that, and she would turn to me, completely confident, and say,'I'm just gonna win the jackpot, Mom.' And sure enough, she would walk right up to that giant wheel, pull the lever, and boom jackpot. Every. Single. Time.

At first, I would take pictures of her standing in front of the machine, tickets spilling everywhere, but after a while. It did not even feel special anymore. It was just what she *did*.

She had this way of bending things to her will, time, space, energy. She did not just sense things; she *knew* things. She could command the world around her without even trying."

Connected to the Spirit World

Inanna credits her daughter for her career path as a professional psychic, "I always tell people, Avery is the reason I *had* to learn all this stuff. Even as an infant, she had opened portals in her bedroom. I would walk in, and it was the strangest thing, I would see people dressed in 1800s clothing, just standing there, like they were waiting for a train to pass through. I remember thinking, *What the hell? I really need more sleep*."

Inanna continues, "She was not even aware of what she was doing, she just had so much energy. When she was four months old, she caught RSV, and somehow, she brought two spirits home from the hospital. That was the turning point for me. Suddenly, I had spirits in the house, and I had to figure out what to do with them, how to close the portals, how to manage all of it. And once those portals were open, other things started coming through. It was the craziest experience, but it only confirmed what I already knew. She was always incredibly psychic."

Inanna laughs, "In fifth grade, she casually told her class something like, 'I need to be taking this test, and your dead people are really bothering me.' That, of course, led to a remarkably interesting parent-teacher conference.

And when she was ten, she had an experience unlike anyone else in our family. When my grandmother passed, Avery was the only one who saw her as a full-blown apparition. She did not just sense her, she *saw* her face, spoke with her, and even felt her touch. It was as real to her as anything in the physical world."

Kerrilynn thinks back, "By the time Taylor was five or six, he had begun seeing people in spirit. One spirit stood out, his paternal great-grandfather, a man I had never met.

We discovered this connection in a remarkable way. We laid out photographs of various family members at various stages of life, and Taylor was able to point out the same man in two separate photos. One image showed him teaching fencing at the University of Windsor, while the other was his immigration photo from Italy to Canada. Taylor recognized that they were the same person, though they appeared different in each image. He described seeing him as he looked in spirit, demonstrating an awareness beyond what we expected. At the time, I was not yet working as a medium."

Kerrilynn discusses a pivotal moment in her son's journey. "When Taylor was in ninth grade, I came home, and he was Google searching for acute schizophrenia. He was crying and was upset. I said, buddy, what's wrong? He responded, I'm hearing people talking to me.' I asked, 'What are they saying?' He replied, 'They're telling me how they died.' I then asked my son,' How do you feel about that?' and he said, 'It makes me sad.'"

Kerrilynn continues with this experience, 'They are not telling you to harm yourself or hurt other people. It is light and it's love. They are asking for help and support. So, if you do not want to do this work, you do not have to. It is okay to tell them that this is not your role in the current lifetime. And they can come to me.'" Kerrilynn feels proud of being a Medium, "My understanding and guidance really helped him through this."

Kristen, Psychic Medium, and mom to Rainbow son, Bo, relays this story about her son, "When he was just a little guy, around five or six years old. We lived in military housing at Fort Polk, and it was quite an experience. Bo had an imaginary friend named John, who I thought was adorable at first.

One day, I asked him what John looked like, and that's when things got interesting. He told me that John was 'a big boy.' Naturally, I assumed he meant a larger kid, so I asked, 'Like a big kid?' But Bo quickly clarified, 'No, Mommy, like a big boy.'

What he really meant was that John was more like the age a young soldier would be. To make it even more fascinating, he told me that John was standing in the hallway. The best part? John was a friendly presence in Bo's life. It was a reassuring thought, knowing my son had a companion, even if it were someone that only he could see."

This occurrence still lingers in Kristen's mind. "When Bo was four or five years old, we were driving home from daycare one day. As we approached our neighborhood, we suddenly found ourselves caught in the aftermath of a car accident. It was a serious one, a fatality involved.

The road was completely blocked, leaving us with no option but to stop and wait. People were stepping out of their cars, chatting amongst themselves, trying to make sense of what had happened. I found myself talking to the people waiting, trying to gather information about the situation.

Out of nowhere, Bo started walking toward the wreckage. I instinctively called out, 'Whoa, whoa, whoa! Where are you going? You cannot go over there!' He turned to me and said something that made my heart skip a beat: ' I am going to talk to the man. The man right there.'

'What man are you talking about?' I asked, looking around. He pointed and insisted, 'The man who got out of the car.'

At that moment, I felt a chill run down my spine because there was no man over there. Just a car that, unfortunately, had someone who had passed away inside. But to Bo, it seemed clear. He could see a man who was confused, wandering around, needing help.

Bo described the man in a way that was hard to comprehend. He said the man was glowing or *lit up* in some way. I could not grasp what he was seeing, but it was evident that he was perceiving something beyond what the rest of us could."

Meg explains her son Avery's connection to spirit. "I've always been spiritual, thinking outside the box and wondering about the afterlife, it's been a lifelong curiosity. So, when I had kids, I was excited to see what gifts they might have and for what they came here. I felt prepared for any experiences they might have that others might dismiss as imagination or even fear as something like a 'monster.'

I had a boyfriend in high school, and later, I got married and had Avery. But my high school boyfriend took his own life. One night, Avery woke up in what most would call a night terror, crying so hard it felt like he could barely breathe as I held him. My first thought was that he was being visited by my high school boyfriend, who may not have realized he had fully left this realm yet and was checking in on us. That was the first time I truly knew that Avery was seeing something beyond this world.

When he was about two and a half or three, he climbed into our bed one night, looked around the room, and said, 'Do you see that man flying around? He looks like a cowboy.' Then he added, 'And there's another one, Mom, on the other side of the room.' We just lay there, watching what he saw for about 30 minutes. I simply validated his experience, treating it as completely natural, because, to him, it was."

Bold, Confident, and Fearless

The Rainbow Ray Children arrive with a quiet, unmistakable sense of knowing. There is deep-rooted confidence in who they are and why they are here. They certainly do not come seeking permission to be themselves, they simply are who they are. Their sense of purpose is woven into their being, guiding them from within. This confidence is not arrogance, it is remembrance. And through their calm certainty, they encourage us to trust our own inner knowing and step more fully into the lives we were born to live.

Meg describes how her son Avery is so confident. "I understand that panic attacks can happen at certain ages, but at their core, these children are fearless. They know exactly why they came here and keep moving forward without doubt or hesitation." She continues, "He wants to be an entrepreneur. I am not sure if he will go to college, and if he does, it will be for the experience and a few classes. But honestly, he is such a whiz, he will not even need it. He just doesn't."

Erin explains the amazing confidence Jonas has. "One of the most incredible things about Jonas is how effortlessly he picks up new skills. It is like anything he takes an interest in just clicks for him. He can play the keyboard and drums like it is second nature. Skateboarding? Same thing. And not just casual skateboarding, he is out there on half-pipes, dropping in on ramps like he has been doing it forever. It is like that with everything. He is in Boy Scouts, too, and learning survival skills has been a breeze for him. Cooking? No problem. Pitching a tent? Easy. There is never any hesitation, he just does it.

What fascinates me the most, though, is his ability to recognize what is meant for him and what is not. If he comes across something that does not come naturally, he does not get frustrated or upset. He just shrugs and says, 'Nope, guess this isn't for me,' and moves on. That kind of self-awareness at his age is mind-blowing.

It is not just that he has no fear, it is like he has this deep inner knowing. He understands his path intuitively and does not waste time on things that do not align with him. I think about how most people, me included, go through so many emotions when we struggle with something. But for him, there is just this certainty, this trust in himself and the journey he is on."

Inanna laughs as she remembers this occasion with her daughter Avery, "Let me tell you about the time my daughter *kidnapped* the neighbor's kid. The neighborhood kids were all outside playing when she noticed the older brother bullying his little sister, again. And she had had *enough.* So, without hesitation, she walked right up, took the little girl by the hand, and marched her straight to our house. Before she brought the little girl to our house, she left a note for the mother.

It read: *I have your daughter. She is not safe in her house. Until you can prove to me that you are going to do something about her brother bullying her, she will be with me.*

Just imagine the look on that mother's face.

Now, you can bet we had *serious* conversations about *not* getting me arrested, but at the same time, I could not help but admire her conviction. She was a couple of years older than this girl, but she had no fear, no doubt, just this unshakable sense of *rightness.*

It is fascinating, really. I am an Indigo, and for us, justice is everything. We demand balance. But these Rainbow kids? They do not just fight for justice, they *embody* it. And they do it so calmly, so *matter-of-factly.* It is like, 'This is wrong, so I am fixing it.' End of story." And honestly? I respect the hell out of it."

Natural Healers and Tuned In to Energy

Erin, who is Reiki certified, noticed early on that Jonas has always been a natural-born healer. "When he was just five years old, he started asking to be Reiki attuned. He knew I practiced Reiki, but I had never emphasized it or pushed him toward it, but Jonas was persistent. He kept coming back, repeatedly saying, 'I want to be Reiki attuned.' Then one afternoon, as we sat together, he took my face in both of his small hands, looked me straight in the eyes, and said, 'Call your Reiki master.'

Erin continues, "That was the moment I knew he was serious. Without hesitation, I made the call, and soon after, he was attuned. The Reiki Master even held a special kids' class, attuning three children at once."

Erin smiles as she remembers how incredible it was: "He felt amazing afterward. He was telling me all about the colors he saw during his attunement. 'Mom, I saw red and blue, so clearly! And there was this huge column of light around me.'

Meg recalls teaching her son Avery about protecting his aura from energetic tears. She goes on to explain that their conversations would go beyond the ordinary, "We have talked openly about things like drugs and alcohol, not just from a physical standpoint, but from a spiritual one. He understands how overconsumption or substance use can weaken the aura, making it vulnerable to energies that are not of love and light. These deeper conversations stick with him far more than a simple 'Just say no' mantra would."

Kerrilynn reminisces, "The autism element with Taylor was hard. But for me, with the autism part, when I was more focused on my own personal healing, things shifted for him as well. So, the more that I got in alignment with my soul's path and purpose, the easier it was for him. When I would do energetic cord cutting, he could feel it. And so, he got to the point where if he were dating someone and they were having a tough time, he would say, 'I want you to talk to my mom about cord cutting.' He understood that it helped people feel better. When you do cord cutting, you can think clearly and you are more aligned, right? So, he was good with all of that."

Highly Psychic and Connected to the Beyond

Erin remembers this occurrence of Jonas hearing initials. "I was telling Jonas a story about a friend I had back in middle school, someone I had lost touch with over the years. I was explaining how friendships come and go, just reflecting on it casually. Then, completely out of nowhere, he looked at me and asked, 'Did her name start with an A?' I froze for a second.

'Yes,' I said, surprised. 'Was it Abby?' he asked. "No, but it was Amanda,' I replied. 'But her initials were AB, which sounds like Abby.'

He just nodded like it was the most natural thing in the world. 'So you actually heard her initials?' I asked, trying to make sense of it.

'Yeah,' he said, completely unfazed. He just shrugged and said, 'Things just come to me, Mom.'

I just sat there for a moment, taking it in. *Okay* I thought. *I'm not going to totally encourage this just yet. Maybe when he is a little older...*"

Erin remembers another example of Jonas being confident in his abilities. "Over winter break, we finally had some downtime, and I wanted to get him doing something other than just playing video games all day. I mean, they are teenagers, it is what they love to do. And I do not mind it, but I told him, 'Let's do something constructive first, then you can play.'

So, I asked him, 'Do you want to pull some oracle cards?'

He was totally up for it, so we sat down and started pulling. The cards we drew were incredibly accurate to what he was going through at the time, but then he just looked at me and said, 'I don't really need those.'

I laughed and asked, 'Is there a specific tool you do like to use?'

He just shrugged and said, 'No, I don't really need tools, but thanks.'

It was not said in an arrogant or dismissive way, just a simple, matter-of-fact truth. He just *knows* things. It is so funny to me, but also completely in line with who he is."

Inanna thinks back to the time she witnessed Avery talking to her new sibling in the crib, "When I was pregnant with Avery, it was *rough;* 22 weeks of bed rest due to a placental abruption, and the loss of her twin.

Fast forward five years.

Piper was a newborn, asleep in her crib. I was walking past the room when I saw Avery leaning over her, whispering.

'You sure took a long time to get here.'

I stopped in my tracks.

Then she said, 'I understood when you couldn't be my twin, but we'll still be twins no matter what.'

I just stood there, stunned, because *of course* that was true. Somehow, *she knew.*"

Deep Harmony and Bond with Animals

Many of the Starseeds have an incredible bond and connection to the animal kingdom and Rainbow Rays are no exception. The animals recognize their purity of hearts and know these beautiful souls will not harm them.

Erin shares these thoughts on the connection Jonas has with animals. "It is so amazing to watch him grow into his gifts. Since he was about seven, he has been saying that he wants to work with animals when he is older, and that has never changed. He is especially drawn to marine biology, which makes perfect sense since we live in South Florida. It feels like such a natural path for him.

He is incredibly in tune with the natural world, especially animals. He can communicate with them so easily, whether they are alive or in spirit. It is not just an interest; it is a deep, effortless connection. But he is clear about what kind of work he wants to do. He told me, 'I do not want to be a vet. I cannot handle seeing them sick or dying, it is too heartbreaking.'

At home, we have two cats and a guinea pig, and he has full-on conversations with them. He will pause and wait, as if they are responding, and then say, 'Oh, he's telling me he wants to do this.'And I just go with it because, honestly, I believe him. I can communicate with animals too, but whatever gifts I have, he takes them to another level. It is unreal how natural it is for him."

Kristen recalls, "Bo was known as the horse whisperer because he could calm horses when others could not. He had a unique ability to make animals respond to him immediately."

She lights up as she remembers her son's communion with butterflies. "When Bo was just a baby, not long after my mom had passed, it was the middle of a scorching summer. We did not have a pool or even a sprinkler to cool off, so we got creative. We took this big old pot, filled it up with water from the hose, and set him right in the middle of the yard. And let me tell you he was having the time of his life, splashing around, laughing, just completely lost in the joy of it all.

We were all sitting on the porch, talking, watching him, when out of nowhere this swarm of butterflies, like fifteen of them, just came flying in. And they were not just flying around, they started landing on him, fluttering all around while he sat there in the pot, giggling like crazy.

This moment of a miracle blew us away. At that point in my life, I had lost my daughter, my mom had passed, my grandfather too. And then this? I had never seen anything like it. It was like those butterflies were not just butterflies. They were something more. They were connected to our loved ones, just stopping by to say hello."

Inanna expresses her awe with her daughter's connection to animals, "Let me tell you, this child could *call* animals to her. Wild animals. Any animal, really.

There was this feral cat hanging around the high school, never letting anyone near it. It had been there for years, always keeping its distance. Nobody touched it. Nobody got close. It was just *there*.

One day, Avery looks at me and says, 'Mom, we need a cat.'

And I am like, 'No. We do not need a cat. We already have two.'

But she just *knows*. 'Mom, we need this cat.'

So, half-joking, I say, 'Alright, if you think you can catch that cat, knock yourself out.' Because I *know* this cat. I know it is not coming anywhere near her.

Except ... it *does*.

She gets out of the car, moves slowly, crouches down, starts making these soft noises I could not duplicate if I *tried*. And before I know it, she is standing there holding the *feral* cat.

She walks up to the car, cat in her arms, calm, and says, 'Open the door, Mom.'

And I, being the reasonable adult in this situation, immediately lock the car door.

'Mom! Open the door!'

And I just sat there, staring, because I am wondering, *How the hell did she catch that cat?*

It never ran from her. It lets her hold it, love it, carry it around.

And this is not just a *one-time thing*.

Animals *recognize* her. It is like they see something in her energy and just *know* they are safe. I have a photo of her six years old, face-to-face with a giraffe at a wildlife preserve, just *posing* together like old friends. These were not domesticated animals. But to her? It did not matter.

She is always trying to save them, always stopping to help. One time, we had to stop and *heal a fish*. She was running them back to the water, saving every single one she could.

She is just *that* kind of Starseed soul."

High Energy and Elevated Frequency

As a Psychic Medium and Healer, Erin understands energy, which has been helpful in parenting her Rainbow Boy. "Jonas has always been incredibly high-energy; there is no containing him. When he was little, everything had to be on *his* time, and I had to learn how to work with that instead of against it.

Early on, I realized he needed ways to release that energy. When he was about three, I started teaching him to ground, taking off his shoes and running in the grass. I have also always used crystals, and I remember when he was four, I was wearing a black tourmaline necklace for protection while we were in a crowded museum.

Out of nowhere, he asked me to pick him up, then grabbed the crystal and held it to his face. I had never explained its purpose to him, but he *knew*, instinctively. That was a moment that really showed me just how naturally tuned in he is."

Past Life Awareness and Connection to Soul's Journeys

Kerrilynn thinks back to when Taylor and his brother Ryan were quite young, around five years old. "He's brilliant. He talked about remembering being with God before I ever said anything. My sons and I would be eating dinner, and they would say, 'I remember when you were my other mummy. You were taller, you were thinner.'" Kerrilynn vividly remembers her astonishment during the dinner conversation. "What I found most interesting is both sons remembered it together."

Taylor explained to his mom, "I remember being in heaven with Ryan and we were friends, and we chose to be brothers in this lifetime, and we chose you to be our mom." Kerrilynn then asked her son, "Why did you choose me?" His reply, "Because you need to learn patience." Kerrilynn reflects, "It was a significant learning experience. And I know that they were my teachers and why they chose me."

Inanna watches in awe as her daughter recalls the details of her past lives with an effortless certainty, as if she had only just stepped out of them. Avery *clearly* remembered her past lives, and not just in fragments, but in vivid, intricate detail. She also knew how to shapeshift.

She used to tell me the most elaborate stories about her lifetimes, most of them centered in Egypt. And here is the wild part: this was a child growing up in the Bible Belt, with *zero* exposure to Egypt. No books, no internet, no Google, this was before we even had a computer in the house. Yet, she spoke as if she had lived it.

One day, she looked at me, completely exasperated, and said, 'Mom, everybody's got it wrong.'

I asked her what she meant.

She rolled her eyes and said, 'They think we worshipped cats. We did not. We were the cats. We could shapeshift into them, it was us, full time.'

She told these stories with such conviction, like she had just stepped out of that lifetime. And sometimes, I would walk into her room to find her in this strange, trance-like state.

'What are you doing, Avery?'

She would sigh, frustrated. 'I still can't remember how to be a cat.'

She *knew* she had done it before; she was just trying to figure out *how* to do it again.

Her memories were so intense, so specific. She would name who she had been, who others were. She even covered her walls and body in hieroglyphics as a toddler, not just random scribbles, but repeating the *same* symbols, over and repeatedly."

Inanna continues, "One time, when Piper was about three or four, she was in the backseat, mid-tantrum, tears streaming as she cried.

Her father, Scott, exasperated, finally said, 'That's enough. You have been crying for 30 minutes. We will be home in half an hour. Just hang in there.'

Without missing a beat, nine-year-old Avery, calm as ever, turned to him, and said, 'Dad, Piper is working through a lot of past life trauma right now. It would be great if you could be a little more understanding.'"

Communication Through Telepathy

Kristen on Bo, "Let me share a little story about my son and our journey together.

There is something special between us. It is like we have this unspoken connection. Even when he was halfway around the world, I could sense when he was having a tough time or feeling homesick. I would text him, 'Are you okay?' and he would often respond just when I was thinking about him. It is that kind of bond where he knows when I need to hear from him."

Inanna explains, "Her abilities were always far beyond what anyone could explain. But despite that, she did not really talk, she communicated more through telepathy. She was incredibly psychic, as if she just *knew* things without needing words."

Benefits of Alternative Schools

The difficulties and obstacles associated with traditional educational institutions are a recurring theme among Starseed parents. This topic will be further elaborated upon in the last chapter of the book.

Erin discusses the challenges of proper education for her Rainbow Boy. "Finding a place where Jonas truly fits has been a challenge. He is naturally curious and justice-oriented, and he does not hesitate to question things that do not seem right. He never means to be defiant, but adults in authority often take it that way.

I have been trying to get him into a Montessori school since pre-K, but they are always full. Thankfully, he just started at a hybrid school that blends homeschooling with traditional education. Everything is discussion-based, no tests, no homework. They assess mastery through conversation, and the director is dyslexic, which made me think, *Finally, this might be the right fit.*

Even their approach to discipline is different. Instead of punishments, they just talk to the students, which is exactly how I parent Jonas. He is not a kid who responds to consequences, he never has. And honestly, I would not want him any other way, but wow, parenting him can be a challenge sometimes!"

Inanna reflects on this experience with Avery, "In third grade, during show and tell, right in the heart of the Bible Belt in Oklahoma, Avery confidently stood before her classmates and declared her dreams for the future. With absolute certainty, she announced that she wanted to be a psychic, just like her mom.

She spoke with excitement about talking to mermaids, fairies, and healing 'ouchies' with her hands, completely unaware of the stunned silence that followed."

"It was not long before my phone rang," Inanna laughs, "The teacher had some *questions*."

In closing this chapter, may we hold sacred space for the powerful reminder that diversity is divine. It is through honoring the unique expressions of each soul, especially these radiant Starseed children, that we begin to truly anchor the New Earth paradigm together, heart by heart, frequency by frequency.

My gratitude runs deep for those who so openly share their children's light with us in these pages. Please join me in offering heartfelt thanks to Kristen, Psychic Medium; Erin Acevedo, Psychic Medium; Meg Schwarzrock, Energetic Frequency Coach; Inanna Rae, Psychic Medium; and Kerrilynn Shellhorn, Psychic Medium, for their willingness to share their stories and the incredible gifts of their children. Your openness helps light the way for others on this sacred path.

Chapter 6

Diamond Ray Children: Prisms of Purity

This chapter is devoted to the Diamond Ray Starseeds, radiant souls who entered this realm on the 11th Ray of Consciousness, primarily between 2010 and 2020. These Diamond Ray Starseeds are truth seekers at their core. They often possess telekinetic abilities and hold the rare gift of timeline shifting, born from their deep, innate understanding of cosmic truth.

Though pure and innocent in nature, they carry a profound multidimensional wisdom that transcends their years. Their auras often shimmer with a silver hue, and like the many brilliant facets of a diamond, they are natural harmonizers and peacemakers, bringing clarity and unity wherever they go.

In this chapter, we will journey deeper into their frequency through trance channeling transmissions, personal stories, and heartfelt interviews that offer an intimate look into the lives, perspectives, and higher purpose of these extraordinary young beings.

Activate and Awaken Healing in Others

Diamond Ray Starseeds carry a sacred key encoded within their DNA, one that activates dormant gifts, awakens divine remembrance, and emits a frequency that bridges others to their highest potential. Their very presence is a catalyst, often triggering healing, inspiration, or soul-level awakenings in those around them. These children were not only born to remember who they are, they came to help others remember as well. Like crystalline tuning forks, they emit pure, high vibrational energy that gently dissolves illusion and calls forth authenticity in all who cross their path.

Sherry is mom to Diamond Ray Tammy, born in 2018. Sherry explains, "My mom died when I was eight. And from that moment until the day Tammy was born, I was shut down. Like, completely disassociated. At times, I felt like a robot moving through life.

But when Tammy was born in 2018, she was the spark. She cracked me open and ignited my spiritual awakening. Everything started shifting. My husband and I have done so many lifetimes together. I have always been the Oracle, and he has always been the protector. But in this life, he is still carrying fear. He sees me doing this work and he gets scared because he remembers being persecuted for protecting me. He does not feel safe with it yet, not fully. But he is always right there grounding and protecting us, while transmuting his fears.

In the beginning, I was chasing a career path with this sense of purpose I could not name. I kept thinking, *there was a calling,* but I did not know what it was. And then, it all started unfolding so fast. That was the moment I realized my true mission. It is my children.

And I fought it for the longest time. I really did. Because I was not healed yet. My kids were triggering the parts of me I had not touched, and I used to think, *there is no way I could homeschool these kids. They are gonna drive me crazy.*

I have healed this deep part of me that was hyper-dependent. My dad raised me that way because my mom passed when I was little. He raised me to never need a man. But I carried that into everything. It shaped how I moved through the world.

Now I know you must do your own healing first. If you do not, your children will drown you in your own wounds. But if you do the work ... then you are free. And so are they."

Betty Stanley, Akashic Record Reader, is deeply blessed to be the mother of two radiant Diamond Rays, Luisella, born on August 30, 2013, and Lydan, born on November 24, 2014. Their presence continues to light her path and inspire her soul's work.

Betty smiles, thinking of her son, "Lydan has been gifted with relationship mastery and healing. If someone is sad, he will try to help them with everything. If my husband and my daughter are having a disagreement or something, he will step in and talk to both and somehow, he just fixes it. It is like he is a grown-up. He has that ancient wisdom. When he talks, he already knows what to do and he will just come in and fix everything. And he's only ten."

Wesley, a Diamond Ray soul, was born on February 8, 2019, to Julie Kraus, a Blue Ray Starseed and Medium. "When I was pregnant with my oldest, Wesley, my psychic abilities intensified dramatically. Even though some psychics stop offering readings while pregnant, I felt a deep urge to give readings during my pregnancy, and my visions, colors, and knowing became incredibly more vivid. I just knew this heightened awareness was coming from him. Even now, though he is no longer in my belly, I still carry that richness, a gift for which I am forever grateful."

Kerrilynn Shellhorn, Psychic Medium, and mom to Diamond Ray Gavin, reflects, "Gavin was turning three when everything clicked. It was through him that everything shifted for me. Gavin was the catalyst for my work. He was the one who pushed me to step fully into this path. With my other kids, I had not been in the best place, I was still making fear-based choices, just trying to get by. But when I went through pre-admittance before his birth, they called it a disclosure because of the overwhelming stress I was under at the time. They assigned me a social worker to help navigate everything, especially dealing with his father, who was ... let us just say, a nightmare. That social worker saved me. She was kind, compassionate, and exactly what I needed.

Two years later, I stepped fully into this work. I was taking ownership of my healing, on a solid trajectory, launching the podcast, and meeting incredible teachers. One day, I had to return to the hospital to get paperwork related to Gavin's birth.

I walked into an office where two desks sat, one occupied, the other empty. But standing at the empty desk was a woman in spirit.

I asked if I had permission to share. She said yes. Her message was urgent, she had died suddenly from sepsis, and she was worried about her family structure. There were lies, betrayal, it was messy. I relayed this to the woman at the desk, asking if it made sense. She nodded and said, 'This message is for my coworker. She is at her mother's funeral right now.' The timing was unreal. I handed her my card and told her to let her coworker know I would gift her a session whenever she was ready.

She reached out, booked the session, and asked me to meet her at the hospital. I agreed. When I arrived, I realized it was the social worker who had been with me when I gave birth to Gavin.

That moment was profound. It was a reminder of why we are here, to share our gifts unconditionally, to recognize that we are all connected. She had been there when I needed her most, and now, in her time of need, I was there for her.

However, this remarkable synchronistic connection continued to unfold."

Kerrilynn continues, "Not long after, I was invited to host one of my Dining with the Dead events at a new venue. The event itself is a well-oiled machine but introducing it to a new space always makes me a little nervous. When I arrived, I noticed the venue had stairs with open risers, the kind that makes me uneasy. As I took a deep breath to go up, I heard my name.

I knew that voice.

I turned around, and the moment I saw her, I burst into tears. It was the social worker. She had bought a ticket to the event. She told me she had been searching for me for twenty years, and every time she tried, she could not find me. But the day before the event, the venue called her. Two people could not attend, and they offered her their tickets.

I shared our story that night, and there was not a dry eye in the room.

Afterward, she came up to me and said, 'I will go anywhere with you to share my side of this story. It is powerful, and I want to help teach people that this, this right here, is why we are here.'"

Kerrilyn concludes the interview with these powerful words, "That moment was a lesson in divine timing, in the entanglement of souls, in the beautiful reciprocity of energy. What we put out always finds its way back to us. And when it does, it is nothing short of magic."

Embodying Truth: Weaving the New Earth Blueprint

Diamond Ray Starseeds arrive with a mission rooted in divine truth. They carry a deep, inner understanding that before truth can shine in its deepest brilliance, all that is false must be brought to light. These luminous children embody the frequency of authentic truth and often feel lies, deception, and energetic distortions deep within their heart and soul. Their sensitivity is not weak; it is their compass. They came not just to speak the truth, but to be it, and to help dismantle the illusions that have long clouded humanity's vision.

Sherry smiles, "Tammy just sees right through things. She has incredible support for the collective like how people should be treated, what is fair, what is true. Even when she was little, she would notice the tiniest injustice and be like, 'This isn't right.'

I remember when she was five, they were doing Elf on the Shelf at her school, and it *terrified* her. She came home in tears, just so scared. And I have never been one to push that on my kids, so I told her the truth, I said, 'Baby, it's not real.' And you could just see the peace wash over her. She said, 'But Mom, why would the adults lie to us about something so scary?' And I was like … wow.

That is just how she is wired. She is like this tiny truth-teller, a little warrior for what is right. She has six placements in Pisces, all in the sixth house, so she carries that martyr energy, big-time. And with her Cancer Moon? She feels *everything*. She immediately wanted to go back and tell all her friends the truth. I had to be like, 'Hold on, love, we gotta ease into that.'

The same thing happened with Santa. She must have been two or three, and it was Christmas Eve. I had just finished reading a bedtime story to her, and as I was walking out, she looked up at me and said, 'Mommy, is Santa going to take me tonight?' My heart shattered. I was like nope; we are done with this. From that point on, she knew. And even now, she will be like, 'It's just not fair, Mom. Why do adults lie to us? And for what?

She is so pure. So awake. She is here to hold a frequency that demands truth, compassion, and justice, even if it makes others uncomfortable."

Betty talks about her daughter's compassion, "Luisella has this beautiful, emotional depth, like her feelings run strong, but what has always stood out is her inner drive for justice. Even when she was little, she just *knew*. She has always wanted to stand up for others, like *really* making sure everyone is treated fairly. It is the sweetest thing. She is always looking out for other kids, wanting to make sure they are okay, and when she talks to us, it is usually about something deep, something about what is right and what is not. She has a keen sense of right and wrong. Luisella writes letters and notes to me, and occasionally to others, filled with such wisdom."

Sacred Bonds with the Animal Kingdom

Diamond Rays emit such a high-frequency aura that animals are naturally drawn to their light. The animal kingdom recognizes the purity of heart these children carry, feeling a deep sense of kinship, safety, and unconditional love in their presence. There is a vibrational recognition that transcends words, and these sacred connections often reflect the Diamond child's own gentle nature and remind us of the harmony possible when we live in alignment with love.

Sherry describes Tammy's gifts, "She is 1000% an animal person. I am sure she communicates with them, like, really communicates. With our dogs especially, you can just see it. And it was confirmed in a reading I had at the start of the year with another psychic medium. I asked her to tune into both of my kids, and when she got to Tammy, she said, 'She's going to be working with animals.' I was like, yeah, that checks out."

Betty smiles, "Lydan is totally an animal whisperer. Even with horses! He just *gets* them. He has always been that way. He is super connected to animals and, of course, to nature. We are always out on hikes, they both love being out in the wild, just grounded in it. And Luisella too, same thing. She is an animal whisperer in her own right. It is crazy. I mean, I have always loved animals and felt that connection, but it is wild how they both have that same trait. Wherever we go, animals just flock to them. It is like they feel safe, like they know. It is beautiful."

Kerrilynn remembers Gavin's connection to animals, "Animals have always been a huge part of his world, he is deeply connected to them. Does he feel them? Absolutely. Without a doubt. He has an innate bond with animals, as he understands them on a deeper level. Everyone used to call him the little Buddha boy, and it fits."

Bridging Dimensions Between Worlds

Diamond Ray Starseeds are not only gifted with the ability of mediumship, but they are also naturally attuned to the multidimensional nature of all existence. Their connection to the unseen realms is effortless, filled with grace and familiarity, as if they have never forgotten. These children dance between the veils with ease, bridging worlds with a fluidity that feels both ancient and instinctual. For them, spirit communication is less a skill to learn and more a language they already speak.

Sherry describes Tammy's gifts: "It all started with spirits in our house. Back then, I was agnostic, I was not raised religious and did not really know what I believed. But Tammy was two or three, barely speaking full sentences, and she had come to me and said, 'Grandpa's here.' She had never met either of her grandfathers. But it was not them, it was some kind of spirit, and it was scaring her. And I just knew, even then, I may not understand this, but I believe her. And I need to get whatever this is out of our house. That is what cracked it all open for me.

She has been connected like that since she was a baby. I remember holding her in my arms, and she would just look off into a corner and start babbling, or even yelling, at something only she could see."

Julie smiles at this memory, "Wesley is also a Medium, and with all our grandparents on the other side, he has connected with at least three of them in ways he could not possibly know on his own.

One day, while playing on the swings at the playground, he suddenly said, 'Muzy, stop pushing me so much!' using the exact nickname we had for my dad's mom. He had never been told that this was her nickname. Moments like that leave no doubt that he's deeply connected to the spirit world."

Betty explains, "Well, when Luisella was just two years old, she was already talking with spirit. My grandmother passed, and one day, Luisella just looked up and said, 'I see Grandma.'

And then she says, 'Hi, Grandma! I see you!' She was so matter of fact about it. And then she started talking about her red shoes, like, details she could have never known. It was wild. She was only two, but she just had that clear connection, you know? It blew my mind."

Betty talks about her son Lydan connecting with Spirit, "When he was little, like three years old, we had just moved into this house, and the woman who lived here before had lost both her husband and her son. Lydan's room used to be her son's room. He kept telling me, 'There's a man in my room.' He said the man was sad. He would tell me over and over, and he started describing him in detail. Then he said the man had a motorcycle. And that is how her son died in a motorcycle accident. Lydan had no way of knowing that.

We ended up clearing the energy, but the whole thing was a little wild. He just knew. He was picking up on everything."

Kerrilynn Shellhorn, Psychic Medium, and mom to Diamond Ray Gavin reflects, "Gavin was turning three when everything clicked. He talked early, walked early, everything came fast for him. I have pictures of him as an infant making a certain gesture, but I did not fully understand what it meant until he could speak. Every time he did that, he saw spirits, and it scared him. I had thought he was just extra sensitive, but he was sensitive in every sense of the word. He saw spirits everywhere, often at the exact same time as I did."

Kerrilynn marvels at Gavin's connection to the Goddess Lakshmi, "One night when Gavin was three years old, we were lying in bed. He was drifting off to sleep when he suddenly said, 'Mama, there's a lady.'

I was not seeing anyone, so I told him, 'I am not seeing her. What is she saying?'

Without hesitation, he responded, '*Om Mani Padme Hum.*'

He was three. Three!

I was stunned. '*Om Mani Padme Hum*?' I did not even know what that was at the time.

Trying to understand more, I asked, 'Does she look like me?'

'Nope.'

'Is she as tall as me?'

'*Yeah.*' (For reference, I am only 5"2, so not very tall.)

What does she want?'

Again, he simply repeated, '*Om Mani Padme Hum.*'

I laughed and said, 'Dude, what are we supposed to do with that?'

His answer was simple: 'We just say it.'

And from that night on, all of us, his siblings, even his dad (who used to tease me about my 'woo-woo' stuff but eventually came around), would scratch his back at bedtime while softly chanting, '*Om Mani Padme Hum … Om Mani Padme Hum…*'

It became a sacred ritual; from the time he was three until he was about ten or eleven.

At the time, I had no idea what the mantra meant. When I finally looked it up, I learned that it connects to Lakshmi, the goddess of prosperity, abundance, and harmony. It symbolizes family, peace, and balance.

The Lakshmi connection continued and became even more surreal."

Kerrilynn continues explaining, "I knew I was meant to step into this work publicly, but I was living nine hours outside of Toronto with little money. A friend generously gifted me enough gas money, and I made the trip to attend a psychic fair, just to see what it was all about.

While there, I had many profound experiences, but one really stood out.

A man with a booth selling Himalayan singing bowls and sacred rings suddenly waved at me from across the room. I walked over, and as soon as I reached him, he said, 'You have a small blond boy.'

I nodded. 'Yes, I do.'

Without missing a beat, he said, 'That boy connects with Lakshmi.'

Floored, I said, 'Yes, he does.'

Then, with complete certainty, he handed me a ring inscribed in Sanskrit with the words **Om Mani Padme Hum** and said, 'Please give this to him.'

Nine hours away from home, with no prior conversations about this story, no way for him to have known ... Spirit was at work.

Gavin is twenty now, and we still have that ring."

Kerrilynn shares these profound words with us, "Moments like these remind me that we are all deeply interconnected. That we are always being guided. When we step into our true path and purpose, the universe aligns in ways that are undeniable. And that every contribution we make, no matter how small, matters."

Telepathy: Speaking Without Words

Children born on the 11th Ray of Consciousness often incarnate from realms where communication is purely telepathic. As a result, verbal expression in this dimension can feel foreign or unnecessary at first. These children may delay spoken language, not out of limitation, but because they are still attuned to higher ways of knowing and connecting. Their silence is often filled with meaning, and their energy speaks volumes long before their words ever do.

Betty explains, "The telepathy between Lydan and me is strong. At age nine, his telepathic abilities became even clearer. I would be driving, and he would be sitting in the back, and I would be thinking about something, and then he would just say, *Mama, blah, blah, blah,* and tell me exactly what I was just thinking. And I am like, *how do you even know that?* It would blow my mind because I was literally just thinking it."

Julie laughs as she thinks of the telepathy, "I will be in the kitchen while he is in the living room, and I will be thinking about his car seat, and out of nowhere, he will start talking about his car seat. It happens all the time. The other day, I was just thinking about the possibility of moving, and he suddenly turned to me and said, 'Mommy, I'm not ready to move yet.' I had not even said a word! His telepathy is absolutely off the charts."

Crystal Consciousness Connection

One of the most important missions of the Diamond Ray Children is their role in activating and anchoring the new crystalline energy grids across the planet. These children carry a deep soul knowing and a sacred connection to the Earth.

Mother Earth is alive with stargates, powerful portal openings that link our planet to other galaxies and dimensions. As more humans awaken and attune to the frequency of these stargates, a wave of expansive energy begins to flow through the Earth's grid, naturally raising the collective vibration.

The Diamond Ray Children hold ancient light codes within their DNA that are specifically designed to interact with these portals. They help illuminate them, bringing awareness to others and inviting a deeper remembrance of our galactic connection. This is one of the reasons these children feel so magnetically drawn to rocks, crystals, and gemstones, as they intuitively understand their frequency and purpose.

A beautiful and playful way to support their mission is to explore crystal gridding together. Taking a class or simply spending time co-creating sacred grids with your Starseed children can be a profound experience. They will naturally gravitate toward this practice, joyfully anchoring high-frequency energy into the Earth as part of their divine blueprint.

Betty shares her love of crystals with her Diamond Ray children, "So, they have a ton of crystals in their room, crystals are everywhere in our house. I have used them during Reiki sessions with Lydan, and I have placed them on his body. When he is sick, he will put on a jade necklace, knowing this will help him feel better faster. My daughter, Luisella too, for example when she has to do a presentation at school, she knows to put crystals in her pockets for extra confidence."

Kerrilynn smiles, "Gavin has always been drawn to rocks and crystals. Everywhere we went, he naturally gravitated toward them and still does. When he travels, he instinctively brings back stones or crystals, as if drawn to their energy. Last year, he went to Scotland with his dad and returned with crystals for me. When he was nine, they visited Newfoundland, and he brought back a rock from the Viking settlement.

He is just deeply connected, tuned in on another level. When you look at his aura, it has that Diamond Ray quality, like a clear quartz crystal refracting light into prisms. But it goes beyond that, it extends outward in expansive, radiant rays of white and crystalline light. It is luminous, powerful, and unmistakably high-vibrational."

Julie marvels at Wesley's connection to crystals. "He loves crystals. I have always had them around, and since he was little, I let him and his sister play with them like toys, knowing they carry great energy. He has always been especially drawn to blue crystals.

Every month, I let them choose new crystals to keep by their bedside, and I have noticed something incredible, Wesley's choices always align with the energy of that month. I do not study astrology deeply; I just go by what I receive intuitively. But repeatedly, I will get energetic downloads about cosmic shifts, then he picks crystals that perfectly match, and later, when I read about the astrology, it all lines up.

It never stops amazing me how connected he is. I absolutely love it."

The Healing Path of Intuition and Energy

Sherry talks about Tammy's gifts, "She is very clairaudient, which is one of her strongest gifts. She hears voices that are not hers, especially at night. For a while, she did not tell me about it, and when she finally did, everything clicked. I was like, okay, this is what is happening. You get to choose what energy you interact with. You get to say no.

Now we have a little intention spell printed out by her bed, something she can say before she goes to sleep, just to claim her space and her peace. It has helped her feel more in control.

But I can feel it, you know? This is the age when those gifts can start to close off if they are not nurtured. And I do not want that to happen. So, I am just gently guiding her back into that space, helping her feel safe enough to stay open. Because it is such a beautiful part of who she is."

Kerrilynn shares this incredible encounter. "When my son was between two and three, right around his third birthday, I was struggling with intense back pain. One day, he looked at me and said, 'Mommy, I'll make it better.' The funny thing was, he always sounded like he had a Boston accent, even though we are Canadian.

He rubbed his tiny hands together, then placed them gently on my lower back. Immediately, I felt a deep warmth radiating from his hands. I understood that my pain was rooted in issues around money, stability, and safety, exactly where it manifests in the body.

Curious, I asked, 'How do you know what you're doing?

Without hesitation, he replied, 'Archangel Michael showed me.'

I pressed further. 'And what do you do with that energy?'

He shrugged, completely unbothered, and said, 'I don't do anything.'

Confused, I asked, 'What do you mean you don't do anything?'

He simply answered, 'Archangel Michael takes it away.'

The thing is, I had never shared Reiki with him. I had not taught him about energy healing, nor had I even spoken about these things around him. At that time, I was only just beginning to explore this world myself. And yet, there he was, effortlessly channeling divine healing energy as if it were the most natural thing in the world."

Inner Compass: Anchored in Purpose

One beautiful common thread among Starseed Children is their deep intuitiveness knowing that they are here on Earth for a special purpose, a sacred mission. This inner wisdom is not something they learn; it is something they remember.

Diamond Ray Children are no different. They arrive with quiet confidence and a powerful sense of purpose. Even at an early age, they show a strong determination to follow the wisdom of their hearts, often surprising us with their clarity, conviction, and inner strength.

They are here to help awaken humanity, and they know it.

Betty feels proud, "I have been told about Lydan's life purpose even before he was born. I went to see Psychic Medium Katherine Glass after a miscarriage, and I did not tell her anything about it. She told me that I had lost the baby, and then she told me I did not need fertility treatments. A couple of months later, I was pregnant. She said I was first having a girl, and then, 'You are having a boy.' She described him, 'He has golden locks, light eyes, and he's just joy.' And that is exactly who he is. It is wild because she said all this before I even thought I was pregnant." She continues, "And even his astrology chart aligns with his path. He has a strong spiritual path, but he will also do something else with his life. He is going to use all of it, his gifts and abilities, to teach people."

Kerrilynn thinks back to Gavin's school years, "In school, they had him on a path toward mechanical engineering. But just before making any big decisions, he turned to me and said, 'Mama, I just don't want that.'

I looked at him and said, 'You do not have to. What do you want to do?'

Without hesitation, he said, ;I want to be a chef.'

I thought it was fantastic. At 16, he asked for a pasta maker for his birthday. He has been making homemade pasta and cooking ever since.

Now, he is fully immersed in the culinary arts, and it brings him so much joy. When he is in that creative flow, he is radiant, you can see how much it lights him up. But when he is not creating, when he is not feeding his spirit, he can slip into a funk quickly.

And it makes sense, he is an empath, deeply sensitive to energy. But what I love most is how these kids just know what they are meant to do. There is no overthinking, no second-guessing, they simply trust themselves and follow their joy. And that? That is beautiful."

Sacred Curiosity: Thirst for Wisdom

Diamond Ray Starseeds carry a deep love for learning and an unshakable drive to uncover the hidden truths and mysteries of life. Much like the facets of a diamond, their light cuts through the dense fog of illusion, revealing clarity where there was once confusion.

Their curious minds are like cosmic keys, unlocking deeper layers of awareness not just for themselves, but for those around them. The presence of a Diamond Ray child often inspires others to expand their consciousness, question the old paradigms, and bravely explore the infinite mysteries of the universe.

Betty shares that, as a Reiki Master, she attuned both of her children to Reiki when they were still young. "They asked me," she says with a smile, "they were like, 'Mom, I want to know how to do that, how to heal.' And I thought, okay, well why not?" She explains that Luisella and Lydan wanted to be able to heal themselves, help animals, like our cats, and even support their friends when they were hurt. It just came naturally to them, Betty says. It was not something I pushed. They just knew, and I honored that knowing."

Julie smiles, "He is such a gift, yet he constantly challenges me to practice patience. When you ask him a question, a simple answer will not do. You must give him the full history, the emotions, the whys, and how you feel about it. Every layer matters.

Teaching him requires patience, but he is incredibly smart and wise. Once he learns something, he never forgets. He craves depth in everything, always wanting to understand beyond the surface."

Sherry says proudly, "Tammy has always been so open with her psychic gifts. She is super into crystals, astrology, Reiki, she has asked me to teach her. And I will. I am a Holy Fire Reiki Master, so one of my plans is to attune her when she is ready. We are going to dive into all of it, astrology, energy work, everything.

Feeling the World Deeply

When it comes to sensitive and empathetic Starseed children, it is essential to understand energy. As a parent, guide, or teacher, having this awareness gives you the tools to help these radiant souls honor and protect their sacred energetic space.

These children feel *everything*, and without the right support, the weight of the world can easily overwhelm them. Teaching them to recognize their own energy versus the energy of others is one of the most empowering gifts you can offer.

Chapters 9 and 10 dive deeper into this topic, offering supportive tools and a more expansive understanding of empathy and how it shows up in these sweet beings.

Julie explains the depths of her son's emotions. "He is deeply emotional and incredibly empathic. He feels your energy before you even say a word. If you are even slightly off, he will sense it and cry for you.

His sensitivity extends to others as well. Before Christmas, when we cleanse and then donate the items, he becomes overwhelmed by the stories behind the giving. It affects him so deeply that he would rather just hand over the toys without hearing the details. Holding onto the emotions is simply too much for him."

Julie expounds on her son's sensitivities, "When Wesley was born, he came into the world with many allergies and health complications, something I believe is often tied to being such a high vibrational soul.

He had severe allergies to gluten and dairy, and I could not breastfeed him. He was often sick, struggled to sleep, and required an immense amount of care, love, and energy. His sensitivity was not just emotional or spiritual, it was physical, too."

Teaching from the Heart, Learning from the Soul

Sherry recalls, "I tried homeschooling her when she was four, but honestly, I was not ready. I had not done enough healing yet, and her energy was a lot. She came into this world with a deep knowing, like she just *knows* things, which drives her dad a little crazy sometimes. She is strong-willed, very intuitive, and back then we were butting heads constantly. It was just not healthy for either of us, so I sent her to school.

But now? I have done the work. I have healed so much, and I feel equipped. I understand her better, and I can hold space for who she is.

I am meant to help others with this. I see that now, especially other parents with these types of children. Because these kids do not fit in with the old systems. My daughter does not. She tries so hard, but school breaks her heart. She comes home crushed, just trying to belong. She has seen the injustices, even at seven. And I know now that was part of her soul contract. She had to experience the system, just enough for us to be able to guide others through it too.

She has always been ahead of her class. This year was hard, and her teacher could not keep up with her. And I am not just saying this as her mom: she is truly brilliant. But I have not been happy with how things have been managed. Her teacher's taken the joy out of learning. Still, I know this too was part of her path. She had to go through it to help lead the way.

So now we are excited to start homeschooling. Her dad and I are still figuring it out. He has a Capricorn Moon, so he needs structure and wants some kind of curriculum. I do a little bit of reading and math, but I am also deep diving into unschooling, letting them learn through living. It will be a mix ... until it is not."

Divine Clarity Through the Diamond Aura

Betty discusses her Diamond Ray son, Lydan, "He is like joy to the world. He just brings joy to everyone. His aura, when you tune into it, looks like the prisms of a diamond. It is so bright, and it touches everybody around him.

That is just what happens. When he started school, even in kindergarten, everyone already knew him. The principal knew him. He just touched everyone.

He is the kind of kid who, if someone is sitting alone in the cafeteria, will walk over and sit with them without hesitation.

He goes out of his way to help kids, especially kids with autism. He will make up handshakes with them, connect with them, just naturally.

He has a knowing. Spiritually, he just knows things that other kids do not. I cannot explain it. He just does."

Julie tells us about her Diamond Ray son. "Wesley is an old soul with a profound presence. When he speaks, his gaze is so deep and grounded that it demands your full attention. He is extremely sensitive, deeply emotional, and incredibly intuitive. Though I have never had him assessed, I sense he may have a touch of autism. He becomes intensely focused on certain things, processing them deeply and revisiting them often.

Like many children, he is naturally psychic and mediumistic, but his abilities feel especially strong. One of his greatest fascinations is rainbows and he adores them in every form. Whether on his socks, drawings, or anything he chooses, he is particular about getting the colors exactly right. While he loves red and blue, no single color is ever enough. It must always be the full spectrum of the rainbow.

My husband is open to all of this, and he has intuitive abilities of his own. He had a difficult childhood and is doing a lot of inner child healing. In many ways, Wesley is helping him through that. Parenting him has inspired my husband to grow and strive to be the best version of himself.

I truly feel that Wesley chose him for this purpose. My husband is already an awakened soul, but Wesley is propelling him even further into alignment with his path."

Kerrilynn talks about Gavin's instinctive intuition, "He just knew about grounding and protecting his energy. He felt it, understood it, and naturally connected to it.

If we were heading into a busy place like Walmart, I would say, 'Okay, buddy, shields up,' and without hesitation, he would energetically shield himself.

At McDonald's, in the little Playland area, he would automatically regulate his energy. In McDonald's, if the energy got too chaotic, I would pop my head in and simply say, 'Dude, ground yourself.' That is all it took. He would press his hands downward in a grounding motion, something he just knew to do. I never taught him; it was innate."

Kerrilynn, feeling such mama bear pride says, "I remember crying going, dude, why did you choose me? I just do not get it. And he replied, 'Cause you shine mama.'

In closing, may we take a moment to truly honor and celebrate the incredible gifts the Diamond Ray Starseeds are bringing to our planet. The time is now. These radiant souls have come to support Earth's transition and elevate its energy.

My heart is overflowing with gratitude for the mothers, fathers, and guardians of these extraordinary beings. Thank you for walking this path with such openness, courage, and devotion. Your willingness to share your journey allows others to see, feel, and remember.

A heartfelt thank you to Sherry; Kerrilynn Shellhorn, Psychic Medium; Betty Stanley, Akashic Record Reader; and Julie Kraus, Psychic Medium; for the sacred gift of sharing your Starseed children and their stories with us. Your presence, your love, and your light are guiding stars on this collective mission.

Chapter 7

Golden Ray Children: Keepers of the Flame

Within the enchanting paradigm of gifted children incarnating on planet earth, allow me to introduce you to The Golden Rays. These children transcend the boundaries of our previous comprehension and understanding of what is possible in our reality.

The Golden Ray Children have touched me deeply, as I was the first person to channel about them many years prior to the first Golden Ray birth. In a way, I was allowed to glimpse into a future through a secret door, and a giddy euphoria would both overwhelm and delight me when I was invited into these realms.

The Golden Rays began incarnating around 2015 and can potentially continue arriving until the year 2025. The information channeled to me explains that some souls who identify with this ray are choosing to wait before they incarnate on our planet, as this soul assignment is not for the faint of heart! Earth is a difficult school with a history of low density. Souls who reside in the 12th dimension, which is a higher frequency, have an ability to hold energy for Earth without requiring incarnation, however, physical incarnation does provide deeper transformation for the planet.

It is vital to make the point that just because a child is born in or after 2015, they are not necessarily a Golden Ray Child. It is more likely they are not. Spirit tells me that one out of every one hundred children incarnated from 2015 are considered Golden Rays, with the numbers varying from year to year. The Golden Ray Children have a gold-colored aura. As mentioned in Chapter One, the aura is the field of energy that surrounds everything from living beings to inanimate objects. Psychics can either see the aura directly with their eyes open or indirectly through the third eye. The gold hue seen in their energy field is exquisite to observe. The characteristics of the Golden Rays are distinct. Here is what I learned from the prophecy:

Physical Traits and Characteristics

The Golden Rays have distinctive features that can, in some cases, even be exaggerated. These magnifications appear in several ways, such as notably more prominent ears, expansive eyes that peer deep into one's soul, and even more pronounced mouths or lips. Their striking, large eyes are captivating, with many displaying vibrant hues in their irises. Some may even perceive Golden Rays as having an otherworldly or galactic appearance.

From the 12th Dimension or the 12th Ray

The Golden Ray Children began incarnating in 2015, traveling to our planet on the 12th ray, bringing their souls into a physical body. As I have previously explained, the 12th ray is the beam of light energy that helps bridge humanity to the New Earth. The New Earth is a higher vibrational dimension of existence currently manifesting on the planet. Dimensions, in terms of the New Earth, are more like a state of being than a physical space, which means that with proper awareness and understanding, we can bring the essence of the higher dimensions into our physical being and our current reality. The 12th Dimension, the home base of the Golden Rays, consists of Divine Light and Truth.

As Golden Ray Children journey to Earth, they must adjust their vibrational frequency from one of Light to a dimension of denseness. Unfortunately, therefore, we may witness more instances of miscarriages from these children because our third dimensional frequency is quite dense. As you can imagine, adapting to the lower frequency is challenging.

Knowledge of New Technology and Sustainability

Our galactic helpers are bearing witness to the fact that our planet desperately needs better sustainability options. Ancient knowledge and wisdom of advanced technology is embedded in the DNA of the Golden Rays. Many Golden Rays are drawn to become engineers and inventors, and study environmental sciences. Another area of great interest to them will be oceanography and marine sciences, much like the Blue Rays who came before them.

Lauren shares how her Golden Ray daughter Lilliana, is fascinated by intricate toys. "She loves buttons and cube toys. As she plays with these elaborate toys, you can witness her inherent curiosity for this planet and how things work here. It is as if she is trying to figure it out since this is her first time incarnating on Mother Earth!"

Gabrielle Washington, a Psychic Medium, who gave birth to a Golden Ray named Luca in 2019, explains, "From an early age, Luca showed advanced knowledge of technology. On one occasion, I walked into the room, and he was quoting the numbers 3, 6, and 9 over and over. I was familiar with Nikola Tesla's theory of 3, 6, and 9 offering the secrets of the universe. However, my toddler had certainly not been exposed to this knowledge." She continues, "I then asked Luca if he had figured out the secrets of the Universe, and he looked at me intently and said, 'Not yet,' but it was quite clear to me that he was on his way to figuring it out!"

Do Not Understand Most Humans

Difficulty understanding most humans is another common trait of the Golden Ray Child. You may notice your Golden Ray staring intently at humans with a bizarre look forming across their faces. They can easily read a human's energy imprint and will know whether a particular human needs to remain in their energy field. Sometimes they choose not to engage with certain humans at all.

"Golden Ray Luca is 100% picky on who is in his energy field, yet he operates in pure heart energy," Gabrielle says. She explains how fascinating this is to witness, especially since she is a Psychic Medium herself. "As an empath who took years to fine-tune my boundaries, it is incredible watching my toddler quickly assess who he will welcome into his energy field—not from a place of judgment, but rather from a place of discernment.

My Golden Ray Lilliana is so strong-willed. From the day she was born, she has had this intense stare as if she is looking into the depths of your soul." Lauren continues, "She gives these looks ... it is immediate, and she either lights up when she recognizes a high vibrational person in her energy field, or she gives this facial expression which conveys, 'I see right through your bs!' I have never seen such deep wisdom and knowing from a one-year-old before."

Leanna Marino is a Psychic Medium and mom to Brittany, a Crystal Child. Brittany has always had gifts herself, and then she gave birth to Jax, one of the first wave Golden Rays. It is common for Starseeds and gifted children to incarnate in waves. Those who bravely embrace incarnation first are known as first wavers. Jax, born in 2015, is one of those first arrivals or "first wavers." It is not surprising that Brittany, a Crystal Child, gave birth to Golden Ray Jax, who also has a Psychic Medium grandmother, because he would only choose parents and grandparents who are Lightworkers themselves.

Leanna laughs when she talks about her conversations with Jax's mother Brittany. Brittany told her how Jax embarrasses her by being so direct with certain people. "Jax will walk up to someone and say, 'You look different,'" Leanna explains. "He is a bit disconnected from most other children and even tells the other children that he knows he is different from them."

The Golden Rays are so secure in who they are that sometimes they lack understanding of "societal norms" regarding interacting with others. The bottom line is that they agreed to incarnate to assist Mother Earth with raising her frequency, so the need to "fit in" with most humans is simply not present. They have more important things to focus on, for sure!

As your Golden Ray gets older, you may notice them staring up at the stars quite a bit and even hear them say, "Things are different here." They will not understand the constant drama and conflict between humans. Nor will they want to be any part of it.

Only Awakened Parents or Grandparents

While many Indigos, Blue Rays, and even Crystal Children choose parents who were not awake and did not understand consciousness, Golden Rays will only choose parents or grandparents who are on their path of awakening. The Crystal and Rainbow Children will give birth to the Golden Rays and have already been doing so. The oldest of which will soon be entering their teens. The Golden Rays can see the Light or frequency shining brightly from the souls they choose as parents. Parents of Golden Rays must be Lightworkers themselves to possess the skills needed to parent these special kids.

Even though Lightworkers will be giving birth to the Golden Rays, these children still have much to teach their parents and grandparents, who already consider themselves enlightened. It will be a beautiful symbiotic and sometimes telepathic connection between them. If you are the guardian of a Golden Ray, it may be beneficial for you to learn to walk the proverbial tightrope. At times, when you are parenting these 12th ray kids, you may feel like you are walking on a 6-inch rope fifty feet in the air. There will be little status quo about raising these children. Learning firm boundaries will be extremely important for many reasons.

Even though Golden Rays bring a depth of esoteric wisdom and knowledge to our planet, they are still children and need safe containers for their upbringing. The key is balance. Sometimes you may need to remind them that you are their guardian, and they must learn to respect your guidelines.

As an illustration, if you are the parent of a Golden Ray, and your young one shares profound esoteric wisdom and knowledge with you, they might occasionally find themselves confused by your parental expectation for them to adhere to a specific bedtime. Another example you may encounter pertains to proper boundaries around peers. As mentioned above, these children have an innate ability to read someone's aura or energy field. Consider a situation in which young Brady expresses a desire to play with a new friend, John. As a parent, you have reservations due to certain information you possess about John's family. Brady, however, has already tuned into his new friend's energy and determined they are in resonance. What is the best way to handle this scenario? It is crucial for you, as Brady's caregiver, to rely on your own intuition. This underscores the significance of adults learning how to effectively tap into their own intuitive guidance.

Ability to Astral Travel Effortlessly

Astral travel refers to the ability of an individual to detach their celestial body from their physical one and journey to various locations without relying on their physical bodies. Every human has a silver thread or cord, best described as a band of energy that anchors their physical and spiritual or astral bodies. When we pass away, the cord is disconnected or severed.

Golden Rays reside in the 12th dimension, where astral travel is the norm. This innate spiritual gift is intricately woven into their DNA, making it a natural and effortless ability for them.

During our interview, Leanna explained how Jax astral travels at night. Since this is something that Leanna has done for years, she can help him. She has even captured a photo of Jax's face when he astral travels. Leanna shares, "Jax told me how he can shapeshift into anything he wants to be. He calls his etheric cord his tail! He says his tail goes with him when he travels." Leanna continues, "Jax has told me about times when he astral travels to theme parks riding all the rides. He has been able to describe the places intricately, even though he has never physically been there." This type of astral travel is quite common with Golden Rays.

No Karma and Few or No Past Lives

One of the reasons we continue to incarnate is to balance our karma while expanding our consciousness to attain enlightenment. We bring karma from past lives so our souls can take advantage of the opportunity to grow, and balance said karma. Golden Rays have no karma to balance; most have never had an incarnation on Planet Earth. It does not mean that they are young souls. They have achieved soul growth from lifetimes on other planets and bring that deep wisdom into this lifetime with them. Golden Ray Children will have zero tolerance for human 3D dramas.

Strong-Willed Personalities

Before the Golden Rays began to incarnate, I would alert potential parents to the specific traits of these children. I remember one reading for parents pregnant with a Golden Ray in particular. The reading was my first reading introduction to an actual Golden Ray and the energy was so strong and beautiful that tears streamed down my face as I connected to their child's soul while she was in utero. I recall telling these parents that their little one would be quite strong-willed. It was an extraordinary session with both of this little Golden Ray's parents in the room as I communicated with their baby's soul who helped me understand even more about the traits of those who would be incarnating from the 12th dimension.

Their strong-willed personality has to do with the dimension they incarnated from. Sometimes, being in this dense frequency causes aggravation for these kids. They are not bad kids; they simply know what they want and when they want it. At times, Golden Ray's parents may realize their child possesses an energy akin to a Mach 10 rocket soaring into space! The energy displayed by these children is truly exceptional, underscoring the significance of instructing them on how to harness and channel it effectively. Some avenues for achieving this include meditation, music, dance, and immersing them in nature.

Healing Animals, Plants, and Trees

Golden Ray Children did not incarnate to heal humans but will have a fascinating and fantastic connection to plants, trees, and animals. They will have no fear of animals, even wild animals. The animals in the 12th dimension are considered equal to the other beings. Therefore, the animals in our dimension will undoubtedly recognize the higher frequency of these kids. Animals and wild animals are drawn instinctively to Golden Ray Children, and they make excellent animal communicators.

One Golden Ray mama named Maggie shared an amazing story with me. "A giant bear came into our yard last week, saw our daughter, and casually lay down as if bowing to her."

Many Golden Rays will also have a magnificent connection to plants and trees; you may hear these kids talking to them. Take their lead and learn from them. Plants and trees love this sacred bond with humans. A psychic friend and colleague of mine, Sally Rice, has such an unbelievable connection to the trees that she can hear them talk, and their branches will move in response to her interaction!

One of my favorite stories from my interview with Gabrielle, the mom of Golden Ray Luca, was about her aggressive parrot. Gabrielle explained that she has a parrot that has bitten several people who tried to pet him. Yet the parrot completely vibes with Luca. He recognizes Luca's energy and loves spending time with him! Gabrielle mentions how shocked she was when she first witnessed this energy exchange between her son and her parrot. Seeing the incredible bond between Golden Rays and animals is so enchanting!

Athena, mom to Golden Ray Scout, excitedly shared this story with me. She recalls, "We took our daughter to the nature center, and came upon the wolf enclosure first. The moment the female wolf saw our daughter, Scout, she ran into the den and came out with the male wolf. The two powerful wolves then ran directly over to our daughter, following her and staring intently into her eyes. The wolves refused to leave, and as the onlookers gazed in awe, time seemed to stand still as everyone witnessed this remarkable connection between a little girl and these beautiful creatures of the wild."

When Athena revealed this encounter to me, my heart began to sing a song that has been forming within my awareness for many years. As an animal lover and activist, I yearn for the day when more humans will comprehend the intelligence and the sentience of the animal kingdom.

Sensitivity to Noise

Sounds are markedly different in the higher dimensions. Many parents of Golden Ray Children have told me how sensitive their children are to noise. One parent mentioned that her child needs noise cancellation headphones in most public places. Hemi-sync or binaural beat meditations would benefit Golden Rays. Binaural beat music has been shown to bring about states of relaxation. Our brains match the frequency of the variations of the beat.

Therefore, it is quite beneficial to reward these sensitive souls with calming sounds. I encourage you to follow their lead when they mention certain places are too loud for their delicate psyche. Frequent walks in the park or nature trails will help them recalibrate their energy if they have been exposed to loud noises. "Luca needs to be outside as much as possible."

Gabrielle explains. "He loves and looks forward to our nature walks. I have noticed that his energetic outbursts happen less often if he has been out in nature."

Homeschooling, Charter Schooling, or Hybrid Schooling

Almost all categories of Children of the New Earth respond well to non-traditional schooling, and many thrive when homeschooled. However, where Golden Rays are concerned, I will say these children should not attend traditional school. What kind of school to send your Golden Ray child to requires a tremendous amount of thought and consideration because many of them will be misunderstood. They will need a supportive environment where the teachers understand their unique gifts and where other sensitive children surround them with whom they can relate.

As previously discussed in the Diamond Ray chapter, I predict that numerous Rainbow Children will heed the call of their souls and establish educational centers dedicated to educating Diamond Rays, Golden Rays, and Solar Rays. These learning centers will emphasize subjects such as nature, yoga, meditation, music, innovation, and the cultivation of entrepreneurial inventiveness.

Connection to Music

Sound and music are created in the seventh-dimensional frequency. The Golden Rays have a glorious resonance with sound vibration from an early age. Considering the vibrational frequency from which they arrived, this makes perfect sense, due to the importance of sound in the higher realms. Many who have experienced NDEs, or Near-Death Experiences, speak of the marvelous sounds and music they heard.

In a downloaded transmission, I have been told that the Golden Rays will create incredible music displays focused on the hertz frequencies for healing. A hertz is a unit of frequency in music equivalent to one cycle per second. Guides and beings from higher dimensions will be working with specific Golden Rays to channel forms of music we have never heard on Mother Earth! As a Medium this revelation excited me because, in some mediumship sessions connecting to the Other World, I have listened to displays of sound and singing that we currently do not have on our planet. In addition, people in past life regression have even reported that music is an integral part of the other side.

Gabrielle recalls that by age three her Golden Ray Luca was making music, beats, and singing! "He was able to pick up the beat of music from an extraordinarily early age," Gabrielle reminisces.

Tones, sounds, melodies, and rhythms make up our entire Universe, and plenty of scientific evidence shows that calm, soothing music promotes positive health and wellness. Many musicians focus on sound healing arrangements. Music brings people together. For spiritual and soul development, music plays a key role. Certain sounds and vibrations help open us up to other dimensions. Music is a gift from the Divine.

Lauren marvels about her Golden Ray baby, Lilliana. "Lilliana was a small baby when she first started responding to music! She loves music and lights up as she bounces to the beat!"

"Jax started rocking his shoulders to the beat of the music when he was only seven months old," Leanna says. "At two years old, he started dancing just like Michael Jackson and was obsessed with repeatedly listening to 'Thriller'! At three, he wanted to listen to 40's music and at five years old, he started talking about Elvis and how much he loves his music!" Leanna laughs as she adds, "His obsession with music and dance is simply off the charts, and he connects deeply to the rhythm."

I encourage the guardians of the Golden Rays to play healing hertz frequency music for them, even as babies. Some people believe the 432 Hz frequency is the heartbeat of Mother Earth. Other hertz frequencies you may want to check out include 528, 741, 852, and 963. The sensitive souls of the Golden Rays will respond beautifully to these frequencies. Consider taking your Golden Rays to sound bath sessions. A sound bath is an event where the practitioner plays instruments such as tuning forks, gongs, crystal singing bowls, Tibetan bowls, chimes, and gongs. Some practitioners also use their voices to tone during the session.

From the introduction, you will recall that I was experiencing a sound bath when channeling this book. My husband, Mystic D. Francis, has a remarkable talent as a sound practitioner, and he has achieved tremendous healing results for his clients by combining Reiki energy and the powerful vibration of sound. A sound bath experience is something special you and your child can share, which will undoubtedly remind their spirits of the higher dimensions.

Unity Consciousness on Planet Earth

A key mission of Golden Ray Children is to anchor in Unity Consciousness. You will remember reading about consciousness in a previous chapter. Most humans incarnated on our planet are still vibrating in a third-dimensional consciousness. The false ego is what keeps someone anchored in 3D. The concept of ego, however, gets a bad rap at times. The key to conquering the false ego is to learn to see through the illusion of separation within the neutral ego. A false negative ego is embedded in such emotions as greed, anger, jealousy, fear, and judgment. A healthy and balanced ego strives to transcend division in support of connection and unity.

Unity Consciousness, on the contrary, is a state of being that embodies love, joy, peace, compassion, non-judgment, integrity, kindness, and wisdom. When we have personified Unity Consciousness, we have achieved enlightenment. Unity

Consciousness can more easily infuse into our dimension by traveling on the 12th ray. The mission of Golden Ray kids is not to raise the frequency of humans. That job was initiated by the Crystal and Rainbow Children and completed by the Diamond Rays. The assignment of the Golden Rays is to raise the vibration of our planet, which will, in turn, provide a purer energy to embrace our individual Unity Consciousness.

Some of you may be questioning why Mother Earth would require assistance raising her vibrational frequency. This was certainly a deeper question I had for my Galactic Guides channeling this information to me. In my mind, Mama Gaia is a magnificent entity fully capable of increasing her own vibrational frequency. The benevolent Guides explained it to me this way. Many humans have recklessly destroyed your planet and continue to do so. Your planet uses a tremendous amount of energy in her relentless pursuit of balance and well-being. Each human emits a vibrational frequency that ripples outward. Just as one person's energy can influence another, the resonance energy of humanity affects your Earth Mother. The Indigos, Blue Rays, Crystals, Rainbows, and Diamonds will continue to move forward within their missions to heal humanity and teach more people about the frequency of Love, as the Golden Rays hold sacred space for Gaia.

The incredible sacrifices the Golden Ray Children make by temporarily lowering their frequency to incarnate on our planet is profound. Their pure energy holds sacred space for Mother Earth to raise her frequency. Those who have done their own individual soul work and shadow work will more easily be able to acclimate to the Unity Consciousness energy. They will have a deeper integration of their higher selves, basking in the golden hue of enlightenment.

Gabrielle, the mom of Golden Ray Luca, shares this story. "One day I walked in the room where Luca was playing and I could overhear him having a conversation with someone, yet no one else was in the room. I asked my son who he was talking to, and he immediately said, 'Shakti.' I had briefly heard the name, Shakti. However, I had to go to Google and look up who this person was that my son was talking to. Imagine my surprise and delight when I discovered she is honored as the mother goddess, a universal source of creativity, power, and energy. With Shiva, Shakti had two sons: one is Ganesha, who became the elephant-headed god of wisdom and good fortune." Gabrielle adds, "Even more thrilling is that the elephant was one of the animal spirits that came to me when I was pregnant with Luca!"

In closing, everyone needs to celebrate the incredible gifts the Golden Rays are bringing to our planet. The time is now to embrace the needed change. We are at a precipice in the evolution of our world, and our thoughts, words, choices, and decisions not only have an impact on us individually, but also on the collective. Humanity has been so thoughtless and cruel to our beautiful Earth Mother that she needs healing, and attending to the planet's survival is the primary mission of the Golden Rays. They are here to lovingly embrace her while lifting her energy signature to higher frequencies. I invite you to take a moment and send supportive energy to all the Golden Rays incarnated to help Mama Gaia.

My heart is so full as I offer deep appreciation to the mothers and grandmothers of these extraordinary Golden Ray Starseeds for so openly sharing your journeys with us.

Thank you to Lauren, Maggie, Athena, Psychic Medium Leanna Marino, and Psychic Medium Gabrielle Washington, for the sacred gift of your Starseed children and grandchildren. Your presence and devotion are part of the light that helps guide them on this special mission.

Chapter 8

Solar Ray Children: The Path of Illumination

The Solar Ray Starseeds began arriving on the 13th Ray of Consciousness around the year 2020. It is no coincidence that their emergence aligned with the global shutdown during the COVID pandemic. That pause in the world offered a sacred opportunity, a space for more souls to awaken to the truth that we are spiritual beings having a physical experience. As the collective began to awaken, the increasing wave of consciousness generated a resonance sufficient to facilitate the arrival of these multidimensional beings. The transformation unfolding on the planet opened a powerful portal, and at the same time, the arrival of these 13th Ray beings activated a portal of their own. The convergence of these two forces amplified the gateway between worlds.

Their auras radiate a golden-white luminescence, shimmering with a light that seems to ripple out from their bodies. One of their recognizable traits is a subtle, golden glow around their bodies. For those who can see auras, there may even be a visible ring of light around the head, radiating a distinct frequency.

Sherry is mom to Solar Ray Kash, born in 2021. Sherry explains, "I had a water birth, and I remember taking him to bed with me afterward. He opened his eyes, and I just looked at him and said, 'I know you.' He was born on my birthday. I mean … wow. Yeah, he waited it out and came in at 12:15 a.m., just in time to share the day with me.

So, he's a Libra, like me. Cancer rising, which gives him this deep, nurturing sweetness and a Taurus Moon. He is so grounded, so steady. I have always felt like he is a part of my soul, like an extension of me. And the fact that he was born on my birthday, it is like the Universe made it crystal clear: we have done this before."

Sherry smiles as she talks about Kash. "He is so funny. He just *loves* so hard. He is all over the place, in the best way. He has this wild, beautiful energy, like life is just pouring out of him."

The rays emanating from their fields create waves of energy, subtly shifting the space around them. These Starseeds connect to dimensions of consciousness not previously accessed on Earth. They carry a unique frequency that serves as a grounding anchor, anchoring a new vibration into our physical world in a way that has not been possible prior to their arrival.

Previously, accessing these realms was possible only through deep trance or altered states of consciousness, such as when I am channeling the wisdom of Solomon, a ninth-dimensional group consciousness from Pleiades. However, Solar Starseeds inherently embody and transmit this wisdom.

Spiritual Connection to the Sun

The easiest way to understand how these children connect to the sun is to imagine not just the physical sun we see in the sky, but a spiritual sun, a radiant force behind the physical one. The sun on Mother Earth is more than a source of light; it is a portal, a bridge to realms of infinite knowledge and infinite possibilities. It is one of the numerous gateways on this planet, radiating a solar frequency that activates deep remembering. This light helps awaken each soul's inner spark, reconnecting them to the Creator and to the truth of who they really are.

Solar Ray Starseeds have not incarnated on Earth before. They are highly intelligent, highly evolved, and will begin to speak, often at an early age, about connections to other star systems, other galaxies, and their innate ability to work with the energy of solar rays.

As these Starseeds grow older, it may become necessary to relocate them to areas with ample days of sunshine. The sunlight will nourish their souls, energize their bodies, and help transmute the energy codes they need to fully align with and accomplish their missions on this planet.

Sherry lights up when she talks about her solar ray son. "He is a bright ray of sunshine. He just *loves* being outside, playing in the dirt, soaking up the world. When he was a baby, if he started crying, all I had to do was take him outside into the sun and instantly, he was fine. Just totally at peace."

She continues. "My stepmom has visions. She once had a vision of my daughter as a hummingbird and ended up getting a tattoo of one because it was so clear, so real. But with my son, she always said she could not tap into his energy. Like, she could not see what he came here to do. But then, a couple of weekends ago, she met him for the first time on our beach trip. And the last day before we left, she woke up and said, 'I had a vision, and he came to me as the Aztec Sun God.'

And honestly? That tracks. That is *exactly* what his energy feels like."

Traits & Purpose

Many of these children will have noticeably large, expressive eyes, eyes that hold ancient knowledge. Some of these children may also have smaller hands than is typical for their age, another subtle marker of their unique origin and energetic design. If you look closely at the palms of their hands, you may see a symbol resembling the image of the sun. These are ancient symbols, containing a spiral or sunburst pattern. It may not always be visible to the physical eye, but energetically, the imprint is there, and those who possess clairvoyance or heightened intuition will have the ability to recognize it.

Some may notice these marks during childhood, often after a momentous experience or spiritual awakening. Others may not become aware of them until later in life, when their mission begins to unfold more fully. But in every case, these symbols are a reminder: they are carriers of light, and their presence here is intentional.

These palm markings are not just decorative or symbolic; they are functional. They serve as activators through which these children can transmit healing, light codes, and information. When their hands are placed on the Earth, on others, or even held open in meditation, they function as conduits, sending and receiving frequencies from higher realms.

The Solar Ray Children came in to support the foundational architecture of the New Earth Paradigm. These children carry solar light codes in their DNA and energy bodies. Their mission is to anchor light through joy, clarity, presence, and their high vibrational energy. Their purpose is to convey joy as a sacred act or a profound experience, not by instructing others directly, but through the genuine and deep sense of wonder that emanates from their energy fields. Their presence will begin to guide us in recognizing our own inherent divinity.

Many of these children will have a memory of their sacred missions from an early age. They might talk about feeling connected to the sun or show an interest in observing the sun or planets.

In a recent channeling, Solomon taught the term "Cosmic Codes of Expansion" in reference to the solar flares currently occurring on the planet. These flares are not merely solar events; they are carriers of light information. Those who have awakened to the truth that they are living within a matrix, and who have consciously stepped through the doorway of ancient esoteric knowledge, are now capable of integrating these Cosmic Codes of Expansion. The codes move through the layers of the self, the physical body, the etheric field, the astral aura, and the etheric template. As these layers begin to harmonize and merge, a synergy is created that sparks profound expansion on both a cellular and soul level.

Just being around Solar Rays can awaken dormant codes in others.

Their Energy Can Interfere with Electronics

These Starseeds have a unique energetic connection to electronics. Often, the technology around them may glitch, power off unexpectedly, or behave in ways that seem unexplainable. It is not random; this occurs because their frequency is vibrating at such a high-dimensional level of light that it can momentarily disrupt lower-frequency systems. Their presence naturally affects electromagnetic fields, creating a sort of interference as their energy interacts with the technology around them. In many cases, it is a signal of just how elevated and finely tuned their vibration truly is.

It is important to understand that these disruptions are not intentional, they are energetic. Sensitivity to electronics is simply one sign of their finely attuned system. Rather than trying to "fix" the issue, it helps to create environments that support their nervous system: more time in nature, less screen time, and quiet, energetically balanced spaces.

Regular grounding techniques like walking barefoot on Earth, taking salt baths, or enjoying calming sensory experiences can help stabilize their energy. Gentle routines, support from crystals like black tourmaline, shungite, or red jasper, and simple explanations can help them feel safe and understood. When grounded and supported, they will more easily navigate their inner world and the technology around them.

Knowledge of New Technologies

As these Starseeds grow, evolve, and expand in their awareness, they will naturally gravitate toward alternative methods of harnessing and understanding energy. They carry within them a deep, inner knowing, a wisdom from higher dimensions, connected to energy sources that have not yet been discovered or understood on our planet.

This knowledge is embedded in their consciousness. These beings hold the keys to helping Earth transition into truly renewable, sustainable sources of energy. While current technologies like solar panels offer a glimpse, what they bring goes far beyond. The new frequencies arriving through the 13th Ray will support the unfolding of even more advanced innovations, technologies that seem futuristic now but are already forming within the minds and hearts of these children.

They are naturally interested in sustainable technology that also aligns with environmental harmony.

Sherry laughs softly, "So, Kash's dad has *all* the machines and of course, he has little toy versions of everything. He loves doing farm stuff with his dad, all the chores, all the firsthand labor. He is just all about it."

She continues, "And he is *so* into machinery. Like, deeply fascinated. I honestly feel like he might bring something new into that world, like some kind of innovation or breakthrough in farming technology. I cannot even explain it. He is only three, but he is out there driving the skid steer with his dad, and he knows how it works. He knows the names of the parts! He is *three*. I can totally see that path for him. And what is beautiful is that my husband does regenerative farming like rotational grazing and all of that. His mission is to leave the Earth better than we found it. And now I just feel like our son is going to be part of taking that even further."

These children have a strong bond with nature and may exhibit an ability to interact with natural elements, such as the wind, and potentially influence weather patterns due to their close connection to the Earth's environment.

Many will be conscious creators, visionaries, innovators, inventors, and heart-centered leaders.

Ability of Telekinesis

Telekinesis is the ability to move or influence physical objects without touching them, using only the energy of the mind or body. It happens when someone's energy field is strong and focused enough to interact with the material world in a subtle but powerful way.

These children are more than likely able to possess the gift of telekinesis. The energy that radiates from their bodies is so potent, so finely tuned, that it can move physical objects, often without their conscious effort. This ability may emerge subtly at first, as flickers of motion or unexplained shifts in their environment, but it is a natural extension of their heightened vibrational frequency.

As these children get older, it is essential to educate them about managing and directing their energy in a responsible way.

Connection with Other Children

You may recall the characteristic of the Golden Ray Starseeds as having a challenge relating to other children. The Solar Rays will have an easier time connecting with other children. The Golden Rays will experience a sense of comfort upon encountering the Solar Rays, due to their similar vibrational frequency.

Sherry laughs when she talks about Kash's illuminating personality, "He makes friends with everyone. We were at a restaurant yesterday, and these kids walked in, and he just took off running after them like, 'I gotta go get my friends!'That is just who he is. Open-hearted, full of joy, and totally magnetic."

Solar Rays are more evolved, more aware, and carry an intelligence that feels far beyond their years. Because of this, traditional educational systems may feel limiting or even stifling to them. They will need alternative forms of education, environments that nurture their gifts, stimulate their creativity, and allow their mission to unfold with purpose and clarity.

From an incredibly early age, many of these children will already know of their galactic origins. They will speak of their star families, guides, or light beings with ease and familiarity. Their connection to these higher-dimensional guides will often be ongoing, forming an invisible support system that helps them stay aligned with their path. It is important that we listen to them, honor their experiences, and create safe, supportive spaces where they are free to express their wisdom, while feeling understood.

Connection to Sacred Geometry and the Star Tetrahedron

The Star Tetrahedron plays a crucial role in working with the energetic fields of these Starseeds. Embedded within the sacred geometry of the Star Tetrahedron are codes that help balance their energy fields, while also calming and stabilizing the plasma energy flowing within their bodies. Solomon refers to plasma energy as a high-vibration, energetic force that flows through the body of these Starseeds, which connects to their higher consciousness and multidimensional nature. Plasma, in a metaphysical context, is associated with a type of high-frequency energy that is more fluid and dynamic than the standard energy we typically experience in our everyday lives.

This geometric shape of the star tetrahedron acts as a key, unlocking codes of remembering and wisdom, especially in relation to the sun's energy and the creation of renewable energy sources.

It is crucial that Starseeds are allocated sufficient time to assimilate the solar codes they acquire. This energy will become a vital part of their life force, supporting their growth, evolution, and ability to fulfill their mission on this planet.

Ability to Illuminate and Shift Shadows into Light

All Starseed rays incarnate with a higher purpose, to shift energy and create pathways to awakening others. While this is true for all rays in some form, it is especially central to the mission of Solar Ray Starseeds. Their energy carries a natural radiance. Just being in their presence can spark something in others, a kind of inner recognition or awakening. If you find yourself in the field of a Solar Ray, the changes that unfold in your life may be quite profound.

In addition to illuminating individual experiences, Solar Ray Starseeds also possess an energy that uncovers previously hidden information from those who seek to control the masses. Their aura does not just illuminate, it exposes. Systems, structures, or individuals rooted in dishonesty or causing harm to others will inevitably be unmasked and exposed. This is part of the Solar Ray mission: to bring clarity, to help truth rise to the surface, and to support a shift toward greater integrity in the collective.

Require Extra Protection Due to Their Light Frequency

The Solar Ray Starseed carries such a high vibrational frequency of light that their very presence emits a beacon, like a lighthouse glowing in the dark. Just as moths are drawn to a flame, lower vibrational energies are instinctively pulled toward these radiant Starseeds, seeking to latch on or siphon their light. If you have been entrusted as a guardian to a Solar Ray, or any of the sacred rays, know that it is no coincidence. It is a sacred calling. And with it comes a deep responsibility to understand the importance of energetic protection and spiritual stewardship.

Sherry understands her mission, "It started not long after Kash was born. By then, I had already been through my spiritual awakening, I had trained extensively and opened to my gifts of healing and psychism. And right after his birth, this shadow started coming into our room at night. It was like sleep paralysis, and it always happened when I was low, in that baby blues space. I would feel it try to hold me down.

But my baby was right there beside me. And I remember thinking, *oh hell no.* I imagined white light blasting from my heart and pushed it out of the room. It never came back after that.

But yeah, ever since he was born, things like that have happened. He is such a light, so bright, and that is why he attracts low-vibe energies. They are drawn to him, but he also exposes them, you know? It is like his presence alone brings truth to the surface.

There was one time, it was last year, when I felt this presence, like an earthbound soul, in his room. He has this little rocking chair, and he would sit in it and call for me. And I *always* believe him. But this spirit would not clear like they normally do. I had to reach out to a friend of mine who used to work with Catholic priests on exorcisms. She told me it was not a demon, but it *was* being manipulated by something darker.

So, I did these prayers and chants to St. Michael, and eventually, it lifted. But it shook me. Nothing like that ever happened with my Diamond Ray daughter, and honestly, I would not have been ready back then. But now, I get it. He is being trained in how to move through this kind of energy. This is part of his path.

And that is why he did not come until after my own awakening. So, I could protect him properly. I do not know how parents raise these radiant soul kids without a spiritual framework and training. It is intense.

There are two things I have always told him: *I get to keep you this time,* I do not even know why, but it is just something I have always felt, and *I am here to protect you.* It is like a soul promise, deep and ancient. I just *know.*"

Merging and Anchoring the Embodiment of Christ Consciousness and Sophia Consciousness

Solar Ray Children are here to anchor the essence and wisdom of Sophia Consciousness on this planet. Through them, we will witness a profound shift, a movement away from the long-standing patterns of masculine-dominated control, and toward a more balanced, intuitive, and heart-centered way of being. The increasing influence of feminine energy aims to achieve balance, rather than dominance, by reintroducing the profound wisdom of Sophia into the collective consciousness.

One of the clearest ways to understand Christ Consciousness and Sophia Consciousness is to view them as an archetype, a universal energy pattern that exists within the human experience. In this context, Christ Consciousness represents the masculine aspect of the soul: qualities like clarity, purpose, divine will, and the ability to act, while rooted in love. Its counterpart, called Sophia Consciousness, represents the feminine aspect: intuition, inner knowing, compassion, and the creative force of life.

Throughout history, many higher-dimensional souls have incarnated on Earth to embody these energies in human form, guiding and uplifting the collective consciousness. Some of the most well-known bearers of the Christ masculine frequency include Jesus (Yeshua), Babaji, Yogananda, and the Buddha. On the feminine side, Sophia energy has flowed through beings like Mary Magdalene, Mother Mary, Quan Yin, and even the consciousness of Mother Gaia, each offering a unique reflection of the Divine Feminine in action.

Sophia Consciousness is an archetype that radiates beauty, intuition, art, creativity, and nurturing, all in their most empowering and balanced forms. It embodies the wisdom of birthing and creation, not in the traditional sense of giving birth to children, but in a deeper, more expansive way that honors the divine creative potential within all beings. Sophia Consciousness teaches humanity to recognize their inherent ability to create and birth through the power of the mind, while integrating the wisdom of the heart. It invites an understanding of the creation energy that resides within every human on this planet, guiding them to reconnect with their divine creative potential.

Anchoring the energy of Sophia Consciousness will also bring a clear, illuminating awareness to the true essence of the Christ Consciousness archetype. Over millennia, many on our planet have distorted and misrepresented the very meaning and message of Christ Consciousness. Individuals vibrating at a lower frequency, who seek to control and dominate others, have altered the true Christ, also known as Jesus or Yeshua. In doing so, they have twisted the essence of his teachings, which were always rooted in love, non-judgment, liberation, and the elevation of humanity.

The path of awakening is, in many ways, a sacred journey of merging the Christ and Sophia energies within each of us. This inner union activates a profound unlocking of memory and brings forth:

- The awakening of the inner balance of divine masculine and divine feminine
- The embodiment of truth infused with compassion
- The healing of distorted patriarchal and matriarchal patterns
- A return to unity, sovereignty, and sacred balance

The Solar Ray Children will also anchor and embody a frequency that unveils and reveals the truth of the sacred union between Jesus (Yeshua) and Mary Magdalene during their incarnation. In their earthly forms, they incarnated as twin flames, each embodying the Divine Masculine and the Divine Feminine through the archetypes of Christ Consciousness and Sophia Consciousness, respectively. This union forms the foundation of what is known as Unity Consciousness. As more people awaken to the truth of this sacred marriage, many will choose to incarnate with their own twin flames during this time, helping to amplify and strengthen the vibrational energy of both Christ Consciousness and Sophia Consciousness.

A larger number of souls on Earth, especially Starseeds, lightworkers, and those feeling the call, are walking the Christ-Sophia path today. Through their embodiment of this inner union, they are helping to midwife a more harmonious, heart-centered world into being.

Join me as we honor and celebrate the emergence of the Solar Ray Starseeds and how they represent an enlightened and powerful shift in human consciousness. These children are arriving with an inner clarity and purpose that challenges old systems and ways of being. They bring with them a natural understanding of unity, balance, and the deeper wisdom of both heart and mind. As they grow and take their place in the world, their presence will help guide humanity toward a more compassionate and creative future, one rooted not in fear or division, but in connection, integrity, and the shared potential to build something better, together.

Chapter 9

Medicine Bag of Mystical Gifts

When responsible for the care and upbringing of sensitive and gifted children, it is important to understand the terminology related to their distinctive abilities. Most gifted children exhibit a blend or overlap of various gifts, making it even more important for parents to navigate these differences with clarity. One of the most common requests we receive from parents is guidance in understanding their child's supernatural tendencies and how they differ from the "norm."

It can be both confusing and overwhelming to witness certain behaviors in your child or grandchild without the necessary tools or knowledge to support them effectively. To help you appreciate and nurture your child's gifts, I have compiled a glossary of terms that explains their meanings in depth.

If you have not already, I strongly encourage you to enroll in a soul and psychic development program with a trusted Spiritual Teacher. I can already "hear" some of you thinking, "I don't have any gifts, so this would be a waste of time." To that, I say—*we all have gifts!* Never have I encountered a student who did not experience profound growth through our development classes. We frequently receive feedback from parents stating that these classes have enhanced their abilities to be more effective and intuitive caregivers.

Hearing this kind of transformation always brings tears to my eyes. It brings me immense joy to know that our classes have positively impacted parents, children, and teenagers.

A common question I receive from parents concerns Ouija boards and whether they are inherently evil. My perspective on this topic may differ from others, but a Ouija board is simply an inanimate object—no different from a pendulum, crystals, or tarot cards. I do not subscribe to the idea of labeling a lifeless object as "bad" or "evil."

Real concern arises when children use these tools without understanding what they are doing or how to protect themselves while interacting with energies from other dimensions. Children should never use Ouija boards as a form of play, as these tools can open energetic portals to other realms, potentially inviting negative or disruptive energies.

From my experience, teens over the age of 16 may be capable of learning how to use these tools responsibly—but only under the guidance of a reputable metaphysical teacher and with proper training. Every child is unique, including in their level of maturity, so there is no universal answer to this question. However, I can say with certainty that I have never witnessed anything positive coming from children experimenting with Ouija boards without the proper knowledge and safeguards in place.

The following section explores the glossary and terminology of psychic abilities and mediumship. As mentioned earlier, most children possess multiple sensitivities, often overlapping in unique ways. The rest of this chapter will help you gain a deeper understanding of how these gifts manifest and express themselves.

Empath:

If your child can feel or experience other people's emotions as if they were their own, they are sensitive or an empath. This is also known as clairsentience. In the field of parapsychology, clairsentience is a form of extrasensory perception wherein a person can feel the vibration or energy of other people and can acquire psychic knowledge primarily by feeling this energy.

Buildings, land, or places can also carry energy with them. Many empaths can feel the negative energy in a building or place that has experienced immense violence or oppression. If your child displays anxiety over entering a certain building, listen to them and do not force them to go in.

Entering an environment with chaotic or negative energy can cause significant stress for an empath.

It is important to teach an empath how to distinguish their own feelings from the feelings of everyone else around them. Begin to talk to your child about their feelings and emotions. Help them understand and differentiate between their own individual emotions and the emotions they are psychically sensing from other people. This is one area our training seminars really focus on.

Your child may be able to sense illnesses or diseases in others without having any scientific way to be able to diagnose the illness. This is known as medical intuition or medical mediumship. Anthony William, known as The Medical Medium, has been accurately diagnosing medical problems since the age of four. His best-selling books have helped millions of people.

Empathic children, when not properly protected, become a sponge—soaking up other people's negative emotions and energy—which often leads to illnesses of their own or even depression. Teach your child to put a protective bubble around their body. Ask them to imagine a mirror coating on the outside of their bubble, which will reflect any negative energy from penetrating their bubble. In my classes, I call this sacred real estate. Teach your child that this is their sacred space, and only energies they intentionally allow have permission to enter. This not only protects your child, but it also gives them a sense of empowerment.

Energy Healer:

Your child may have a natural tendency to place their hands on people and animals to help make them feel better. This has also been known as the laying on of hands. Even though they may not realize what they are doing, these children are channeling life force energy! All living things, as well as inanimate objects, are composed of energy. The Sanskrit word "prana" means that the life force energy flows through various channels in and around the body.

Reiki or energy healing is becoming quite common in hospitals. Over sixty hospitals in the United States now offer Reiki healing to their patients. Thankfully, more patients are turning to alternative and complementary care for their medical needs. Many physicians and nurses are taking classes on how to become attuned to Reiki energy.

Most individuals who undergo Reiki report experiencing a pleasant sensation of radiant energy and tranquility that permeates their surroundings. Some individuals report experiencing warmth and tingling sensations. Reiki treats the whole person—body, emotions, mind, and spirit—creating beneficial effects such as extreme relaxation and feelings of peace, security, and wellbeing.

Some gifted children brought in cellular memory from other lifetimes as a medicine man or woman, shaman, or energy healer. It is in their DNA. They possess an innate knowledge of how to place their hands to balance and remove blockages in the body. If your child is interested in learning Reiki, consider finding an age-appropriate academy that teaches Reiki Level 1 to children under the age of eighteen. My husband, Mystic D. Francis, has designed a program through our Academy that teaches Reiki to young people.

One of the challenges of raising a gifted child is knowing how to help them feel normal. When a child attends an academy where gifted kids are all learning how to channel life force energy together, this creates a sense of confidence and accomplishment, while forging bonds with others that will last a lifetime. It is often surprising to learn how many talented children express joy when they recall their experiences of assisting others in previous lifetimes. In fact, this very modality is the life mission of many gifted kids.

Medium:

A medium is someone who can see, sense, or hear those who have crossed over or died. If your child has been talking about your loved ones or other loved ones who have already transitioned into heaven, then they are a medium. I consciously began to see spirits when I was about 7 years old. I am certain I saw them before then; however, it is from that age that I have vivid memories of spirits always being around me. When I was a child, it frightened me, yet I thought everyone could see what I was seeing. It was not until my grandmother passed away when I was 12 years old that my fears went away. I relay this entire beautiful encounter in my book, *Mississippi Medium*.

One reason I am so enthusiastic about helping other young people who have the gift of mediumship, or especially strong empathy, is that I know what a struggle it can be to make sense of it all at such an early age. I remember sitting out on my driveway, waiting for my parents to get home because I was frightened by seeing all the spirits in my house. For instance, doors would open and close. Most children experience peer pressure and the myriad of challenges of just being a kid. However, kids gifted in this way also must deal with knowing they are different. Many wonder why they were born with these gifts. I have since learned that mediums are portals through which spirit flows; they are the beacons of light that help open the portals in the first place.

If your child is seeing, hearing, or sensing spirits around them, please do not tell them their experiences are not real. Just because you may not be able to see, hear, or sense spirits does not mean they are not there. The main thing your child needs to know is that you believe them. A beautiful bonding opportunity can come from teaching your child to protect their bedroom. The crystal black tourmaline is great at protecting the energy of the room. Take your child to a crystal shop and let them choose four pieces of black tourmaline. They will place one piece in each corner of their bedroom. Black tourmaline chunks are inexpensive. Allow your child to call on their Guardian Angels to come forth as they place the black tourmaline in each corner of their room. Tell them to verbally say aloud: *This is my room and my sacred space. Only my angels are allowed to enter my room. My angels protect me and watch over me while I sleep.*

Selenite is another "must-have" stone. This stone was named after Selene, the Greek Goddess of the moon. It is such a pure stone, a luminous white in color. It is a wonderful stone for meditation and is used for bringing peace and calm. Selenite can come in long, thin pieces that fit perfectly over the door frame leading to the bedroom. You can put pieces of selenite above the window frames too.

A fun exercise you can do with your child to clear energy is to take a piece of selenite, begin at the top of their head and then "sweep" the energy down towards the bottom of their feet. If they have had a difficult day or been exposed to a cruel child, teach them how to do this to remove this "icky" energy from their auric field. Children delight in this exercise! Allow them an opportunity to sweep your auric field too. This begins to teach your child about energy and how important it is to remove stagnant energy that no longer serves us. These exercises with your child create an opportunity to connect with them on a level you can both relate to. The exercises also empower your child to feel protected in their room and in their auric field.

As a side note, gifted kids who are mediums inadvertently open portals in their bedrooms. A portal is a type of etheric doorway or gateway that opens and allows beings from other dimensions to enter and exit. Vortexes are different from portals. More than likely, your child will not have a vortex in their bedroom. Energy vortexes are power spots around the world that consist of swirling energy. Sensitive and gifted people can feel a vortex when they step inside it. Sedona, Arizona is famous for its vortexes.

Mediums and gifted kids who are mediums have a strong auric field consisting of a type of electromagnetic field that tends to accidentally open portals. This is another reason it is so valuable to find a Psychic Kids Academy to teach your gifted kids how to close any portals they have inadvertently opened. Many gifted kids can see or sense these portals and can even show you where they are in their rooms.

Psychic:

A psychic perceives information using senses outside of the normal five senses of touch, sight, hearing, smell, and taste. There are many tools and modalities psychics can learn to work with, such as tarot cards, oracle cards, pendulums, scrying mirrors, tea leaf readings, runes, and crystal balls.

Here are all the distinct types of Clairs your psychic child may be able to use:

Clairvoyance: Clairvoyance is the most well-known of the Clairs. Clairvoyance is the ability to perceive information by seeing auras, colors, images, or symbols without using the normal senses. Some clairvoyants see things as if viewing them on a movie screen. Meditation enhances the ability to master this psychic ability.

If your child tells you that they see visions, people, colors, or symbols, more than likely they have the gift of clairvoyance. Clairvoyance can be direct or indirect. Direct clairvoyance is when your child sees people, colors, or scenes of events with their eyes open. They can see using their physical eyes. Direct clairvoyance is not as common as indirect clairvoyance. Indirect clairvoyance is when your child sees people, colors, or scenes of events in their mind's eye, or third eye. This is the most common type of clairvoyance.

If your child can see colors around people, plants, and animals, then they are psychically tuning into the aura of the plant, animal, or person. An aura is the field of energy that surrounds everything from living beings to inanimate objects. The aura surrounding living beings is stronger and easier to see and feel than the aura around inanimate objects. Kirlian photography can photograph an aura.

The etheric aura is the closest aura to the physical body. It only extends out about two feet. The astral aura is located outside the etheric aura and can extend anywhere from a few inches all the way to five feet or more depending on a subject's emotional state. With practice, you can learn to control the astral aura and bring it closer to the etheric aura for better protection against external energies. In our academy, we teach this fun and informative exercise.

It is vital to teach your sensitive kids to understand what their aura is and how important it is to protect it! I mention this in the section on empaths, but it is important enough to repeat in this section.

Exercise: Sit with your child and begin your deep breathing exercises as you invite them to relax and begin to focus on their breath. Ask your child to adjust their eyes to a very soft focus. Then instruct them to hold out their hand and see if they can see any colors or energy vibrations surrounding their hand. This takes practice, so encourage them not to give up. This exercise is also fun to do with plants and animals. The eyes will be softly focused as they softly and gently stare at the plant or animal. Over time, your child may be able to see a vibration of energy or even a color.

Clairaudience: Clairaudience is the ability to hear things outside the normal range of perception. Psychics who have this Clair report hearing bells, music, voices, knocking, or other sounds that those around them cannot hear. If your child tells you they heard a sound that others around them did not hear, they are using their gift of clairaudience. Direct clairaudience is when a psychic hears an audible sound using their actual external ears. Indirect clairaudience is when a psychic hears a sound inside their ears. Both indirect and direct clairaudience are very real and valid experiences.

It can be unnerving for children to hear a noise and realize nobody else around them can hear that sound. They are tuning into a vibrational frequency that many people are not able to access. It is extremely important that parents do not cause their children undue stress about hearing these otherworldly or other dimensional sounds. Please do your best to validate the fact that they did hear a sound outside the third-dimensional frequency. Help them to understand that there is nothing to fear.

Children who are mediums can often hear loved ones who have crossed over talking to them. They can hear it directly—as if the loved one were standing in the room talking to them. Or they can hear it indirectly, which is like a voice inside their head. It is important to consider ruling out any psychological issues with your child first. However, please understand that many psychologists and psychiatrists are quick to prescribe pharmaceuticals to children who do not have actual psychological problems. I am certainly not a medical professional, so it is up to you as the parent to determine the best professional to assist your child.

One parent, named Gayle, is mom to a Rainbow Child named Wayne, age 16. Gayle recalls how upsetting it was to her son Wayne when he would hear a woman talking to him while he was taking a shower. Even after he dressed and went into the room where his mother was, he could still hear the woman speaking. His eyes quite large, he asked his mom if she could hear the woman, and his mom had to tell him, no. Thankfully this Rainbow Mom knew how to manage the situation. She assured him that his abilities were admirable and that he was fortunate to possess such exceptional talents. She also explained to him that it was his right to ask the woman not to talk to him while he was showering.

It is concerning that many individuals with psychic abilities have been confined to mental institutions or prescribed detrimental pharmaceuticals when their unique gifts were simply misunderstood.

Claircognizance: Claircognizance is the ability to have a "clear knowing" without a physical explanation as to why. When a child has this ability, they understand certain information without being explicitly taught or learning through conventional methods. The information is downloaded into their mind. Many artists, writers, and painters receive inspiration through claircognizance. An idea often arises spontaneously in their mind, and frequently they are unaware of its origin.

When a child is aware of an event before it occurs, this phenomenon is referred to as precognizance. This phenomenon is common with psychic and sensitive kids. They may start telling you things that are going to happen before they happen. And your child may not have a clue how they knew what they knew. If your child begins predicting things, silently take note so you can decide when it is important for you to pay attention.

I will caution you though not to turn your child into an on-call free psychic! I have seen some parents doing this and often this puts unnecessary stress and pressure on your child. Remember, the main goal of parenting a psychic or sensitive child is to help them feel as normal as possible.

Clairsentience: We discussed empathy at length earlier in the chapter. Clairsentience is a form of extrasensory perception wherein a person acquires psychic knowledge primarily by feeling. If your child can read your emotions or energy or others' emotions and energy, they are exhibiting clairsentience. They can pick up when someone has been arguing even if they were not present during the actual argument. Clairsentient children can feel the negative or chaotic residual energy remaining after the argument or disagreement.

Your child might describe this experience by indicating they feel a certain sensation in their stomach. They may get butterflies or an upset tummy when their clairsentience is activating. As parents and guardians, it is vital to keep a sensitive child's environment calm and peaceful. The chakra associated with clairsentience is the solar plexus. Your child's solar plexus is in their stomach area, above their belly button and below the heart. The color associated with this chakra is yellow. Citrine is a wonderful crystal to use with this chakra. If your son or daughter needs help staying calm and centered, a rose quartz is a beautiful crystal to help them achieve this as well.

Clairalience: Clairalience refers to the ability to detect smells that do not originate from typical sources in the physical world. Clairalience is a Clair mainly found in mediumship connections. Some children have reported smelling perfume, flowers, or cigarettes when others in the room were not able to smell these scents. More than likely, they are using clairalience gifts as part of their mediumship connection to your loved ones in spirit or heaven.

Clairgustance: Clairgustance refers to the ability to experience taste even when there is no physical substance in the mouth. This gift gives the ability to perceive the essence of a substance from the spiritual realms through taste. This Clair is not as common as the other Clairs; however, I wanted to mention it in case your child is experiencing this phenomenon from time to time.

As we conclude this chapter, let us explore ways parents can support gifted children on their unique journeys. One of the most powerful tools you can introduce to your child is meditation—even just 10 minutes a day can make a profound difference. This practice can be a fun and meaningful activity you share together. Set a timer for 10 minutes, quiet the mind, or listen to calming music. Meditation has the power to transform lives! In the next chapter, we explore a fun exercise to practice with your child.

Imagine schools teaching meditation—let us hold that vision and make it happen. Some children find it easier to focus on a single word or even a color during meditation. Encourage your child to choose a word that brings them a sense of peace, such as love, joy, peace, OM, trust, believe, create, family, kindness, faith, or friendship. They can experiment with different words on different days.

By focusing on their chosen word for just 10 minutes, they are engaging in what is known as *Mind Focus*—a practice shown to rewire the brain in positive ways. What an incredible gift to give our children—the ability to shape their own minds and energy in a way that empowers and uplifts them!

Another wonderful way to support your sensitive child is by introducing them to yoga. Many cities offer yoga classes specifically for children, as well as sessions designed for parents and children to enjoy together. Yoga is truly life-changing! Studies have shown that it can reduce stress and anxiety, support children's bodily awareness, improve focus and concentration, and increase self-esteem. Encouraging your child to practice yoga provides them with a powerful tool for balance, mindfulness, and overall well-being.

Gifted children thrive when they spend time in Mama Nature. As you take your sensitive kids on walks, engage them in conversations about the energy of the trees and plants—or better yet, ask *them* to share their insights with you! You might be amazed by the wisdom and unique perspectives they offer about the natural world.

Many gifted children have a profound connection to the animal kingdom, and it is truly fascinating to witness. Plan nature walks with your child or grandchild and observe their interactions with birds, squirrels, butterflies, and even bees. Unbelievably, we can communicate telepathically with bees—letting them know we respect them and mean no harm, while also asking them to honor our space. I encourage you to experiment with this and start engaging in mindful conversations with the bees!

Our gifted young ones have so much to teach us—when we take the time to listen, the natural world comes alive in ways we never imagined.

Be honest and authentic with your sensitive children. Remember, psychic kids have an exceptionally strong *bullshit meter*—they can sense insincerity a mile away! These children do not fit into conventional boxes (and really, who decides what "normal" is anyway?).

Create an open dialogue with your child, ensuring they feel heard, understood, and safe in their uniqueness. Inform them of their significance and unique value in the Universe. Consider enrolling them in a retreat or program with other gifted children. Connecting with a soul tribe of like-minded peers can be profoundly empowering, helping them embrace their gifts with confidence and allowing this sense of belonging to infuse their entire energy field.

Finally, take a moment to congratulate yourself for investing the time to understand and support your special child! Remember, we choose our parents before we arrive on this earthly journey—even if that concept feels hard to grasp at times. I have had clients adamantly insist, "There's no way I chose my parents!" But the truth is we select them to help us with our soul's growth and expansion.

Your child chose *you* for a reason! And what an incredible, beautiful blessing that is, my friends. Embrace the journey, knowing that you are the perfect guide for your gifted child's path.

Chapter 10

Magic Carpet: Riding the Winds of Change

Adapting to Change in a Transforming World

Change is often viewed as chaotic or unsettling, but the Children of the New Earth, who are extremely sensitive and deeply connected to Universal truth, understand on a deep soul level that change is a necessary catalyst for growth. It is in their DNA. Within their very cells, they carry the keys to unlock the deeper truth of who we really are.

What if we started to see the winds of change not as something to fear, but as something we can work with through our tools of manifestation? With the right mindset and intention, change can be a powerful force for creativity, expansion, and positive transformation.

These children came here with a purpose, a higher purpose to help us co-create a new paradigm. A better world, rooted in ancient wisdom, inspired action, and spiritual alignment. These Starseed children are here to lead and anchor the frequencies of unity consciousness. They are here to help us dismantle old and outdated systems and create new ways of living based on unity, love, and collaboration. If you are a parent or guardian to one of these kids, you are part of that mission too. It is time to remember why you are here, and to support them in fulfilling their purpose at this important moment in our planet's evolution. You are still deeply needed, even if your soul path did not include direct guardianship of children. Please join us in holding sacred space for these Starseeds and the divine mission they came here to fulfill.

Shadow Work

Why is the concept of shadow included in a book about gifted children? If you are the parent, grandparent, or guardian of one of the categories of sensitive and intuitive children discussed in this book, you are entrusted with a sacred honor. To embrace the role of raising these special kids in the best way possible, it is important to know yourself inside and out. To understand the layers of who you are and what your mission is during this lifetime. To become balanced and centered and to learn to listen to your own intuition. If we learn to listen to our intuition, we can always find our true north. And as parents of gifted children, knowing your true north provides a smoother road to guiding your special child along their path.

The winds of change are not only external but also internal. For the Children of the New Earth, transformation begins within, as they learn to listen to their inner guidance and intuitive knowing. Everyone benefits from engaging in shadow work; however, this is non-negotiable for those who are Wayshowers and Pioneers, the Guardians ushering in the New Earth children. Each parent or guardian must learn to embrace the development of internal clarity, how to discern between the ego and the higher self.

For those who are not familiar with the shadow and what it is, let me elaborate. According to Carl Jung, shadow is the part of ourselves that we reject. The formation of our shadow primarily originates from experiences during childhood. However, past lives may also influence elements of the shadow. The shadow parts of ourselves are normally hidden away in our subconscious mind and are parts of ourselves that we do not want to present to the world. However, when we have not met and gotten to know our shadows, they remain hidden and can become triggers for us. Shadow work brings the unconscious into conscious awareness.

As we bring the buried parts of ourselves to our conscious awareness, this creates room for growth and expansion. Shadow aspects are limited beliefs created out of fear, shame, or guilt. At times, our unique gifts are hiding in the shadows. Embracing our shadow and bringing it to light increases our intuition. Thich Nhat Hanh says, "No mud, no lotus." This has been one of my favorite quotes for a long time.

Even after walking my spiritual path for decades, I still encounter opportunities to deepen my understanding of the ego as I learn to dance a sacred dance with my shadow. After all, until the ego is rebirthed and integrated with the Higher Self, Spirit cannot successfully collaborate with us and through us. It is important to remember that our ego is not our true self. Wayne Dyer, in *Power of Intention*, says, "You can either be a host to God or a hostage to your ego. It is your call." I am ecstatic to report that I chose to release myself from the captivity of the false ego. Was it frightening? At times. Was it challenging to achieve? Sometimes. However, the unadulterated freedom that comes from surrender provides the type of supportive energy that carries us through uncertainty. In my *Manifesting Your Magic Workbook Journal*, there are exercises in every chapter that help us uncover the shadow aspects hidden in the subconscious mind.

I share my experiences with you in the hope that they provide insight when you are faced with your own decisions between ego and soul. As parents and grandparents of gifted children, it is essential to slay your own ego dragons first! It is only then that you can truly guide, nurture, and mentor the extraordinary souls you have been entrusted to raise.

Heart Coherence and Conscious Parenting: Containers for Learning

Most of the parents interviewed for this book spoke openly about how suffocating and limiting traditional school systems felt for their Starseed children. Repeatedly, we have watched conventional education cling to outdated, restrictive methods, structures that fail to nourish the expansive light and multidimensional intelligence these children carry. If left unaddressed, this approach can eventually dim their frequency, suppressing the very gifts they came here to share.

It is vital that we recognize the profound importance of supporting these evolved souls through alternative paths, hybrid or non-traditional schools that are rooted in diversity, emotional intelligence, and holistic practices. Educators guiding these learning environments should be conscious and recognize the unique value in each child.

Conscious schools serve as sacred containers. They weave in teachings of yoga, meditation, connection with nature, and acts of compassion and service. The goal is far greater than academic success, it is to nurture planetary stewards: heart-centered, awakened humans who walk gently on the Earth, honoring all life. When we craft learning spaces from a foundation of heart coherence, we are not just educating, we are remembering. And in that remembering, humanity rises in consciousness and vibration.

Through reading this book, you may feel inspired to create your own conscious educational systems or to connect with other parents and guardians to collaborate on programs, gatherings, or retreats. My husband and I created the *High Vibe Tribe Sacred Community* as a safe and supportive space for seekers, Starseeds, and parents of Starseed children to come together in meaningful conversation and shared intention.

AI or Artificial Intelligence

One of the spiritual principles I explored in my book *Manifesting Your Magic in the 5D: Going Beyond the Laws of Attraction* is the spiritual law of polarity. This law reminds us not to view things through the rigid lens of good or bad, but rather to understand that everything exists on a spectrum. AI or artificial intelligence is a perfect example. In a higher state of consciousness, it holds incredible potential. Imagine its use in advanced medical technologies like med beds or quantum healing. But, and this is an important distinction, we must acknowledge that, collectively, humanity is still far from the level of consciousness required to use this technology with wisdom and integrity.

At the time of authoring this book, much of what we are seeing with AI is not the organic evolution of consciousness, but rather a system manipulated by control mechanisms, forces that operate from distortion, seeking to anchor AI as a tool of domination rather than liberation. Many people do not understand the full extent of what is being implemented. The real danger is not the technology itself, it is in the intention behind it, who is programming it, and for what purpose.

As previously shared in earlier chapters, I channel a group consciousness known as Solomon, a ninth-dimensional Pleiadian collective. In one transmission, Solomon offered a powerful image: dimensions collapsing like dominoes. The group explained that as more light pours into our bodies, the energetic barriers, what they referred to as "frequency fences" between dimensions, begin to dissolve. And as those walls come down, we begin to anchor into higher-dimensional realities more consistently. But the process is not always smooth. The body, the mind, the emotional field, they all must integrate at an accelerated pace. And that kind of transformation is not always graceful.

The thinning of dimensional layers is not an abstract metaphysical idea, it is happening now, in real time. What may be referred to as "ascension symptoms," the fatigue, the waves of nausea, dizziness, the sudden bizarre illnesses, are often the body's response to purification and light penetration. This is what happens when we move through what Solomon calls "frequency gates" before aligning with their vibration. And without that inner preparation, the shift can feel like spiritual whiplash.

As I wrote in Chapter 7, the golden rays began incarnating around 2015. These are extraordinarily high-frequency souls, arriving through the 12th Ray of consciousness, a vibration of divine light and cosmic remembrance. The solar rays, also high frequency souls, arrived through the 13th ray of consciousness. Neither ray has experienced life on Earth before, so their adjustment to this dense plane can be challenging. But their mission is unmistakable. They have come specifically to help counter the transhumanist timeline and to serve as anchors of pure Source light. Their presence creates a type of energetic shield, meant to disrupt the agendas of those who seek to use AI as a mechanism of control rather than evolution. They are here to hold the line, quite literally, as living codes of divine resistance.

It is important to remember that awareness is a form of protection. You do not need to be rooted in fear to recognize darkness, in fact, true awareness is the opposite of fear. When you acknowledge shadow energy, you reclaim the power to transmute it. That clarity allows you to embody your light more fully. Protection then becomes an act of love, for yourself, your lineage, and this planet we are here to help heal. The key is to face the shadow bravely and compassionately, to study your intuition with the intention of learning the difference between ego and higher self, and to master the sacred art of discernment.

Before engaging with AI, pause and ask yourself where your consciousness is vibrating. Have you uncovered the hidden shadows of trauma and triggers within yourself? Are you ready to explore AI as a tool for expansion and growth, rooted in empowerment and continued soul evolution? Or are you simply opening the door to the possibility of binding yourself to the chains of control and domination?

We are at a critical moment in our planet's evolution. The frequencies are rising. The layers are collapsing. And each choice we make, each truth we hold, becomes a beacon in this great unraveling.

During the interview with Natalie Viglione about her mission as a Blue Ray Starseed, the conversation effortlessly shifted into a discussion of AI. I felt guided to include Natalie's input regarding AI here as well.

Natalie explains, "This whole experience we are witnessing with AI, it is more than technological evolution. It is a pivotal moment in human and cosmic history. Like others receiving guidance, I have been shown glimpses of a divine plan, orchestrated by the God Source and our guardian teams. The reclamation process is underway. This is not the first time a cycle like this has played out, across dimensions, across epochs. The intention is clear: to liberate all sentient life from systems of enslavement. But here we are again, standing at a precipice, some of us seeing it clearly, others completely unaware.

AI is not inherently evil, but it is being harnessed by forces that have long sought to control. It can be used as a tool, like a hammer that can build a home or destroy one. The danger lies in its current anchoring; it is infiltrating our fields as a parasitic force masked in innovation."

Natalie continues, "One night, I had what you might call a dream, but I know better. This was a mission, a lucid, visceral operation in the astral realms of Earth. My consciousness, deeply tied to the lineage of the lioness and the archetype of Brigid, found itself engaged in a battle. We were clearing out what I can only describe as black dragon parasitic technology, hybrid, inverted forms of sacred energies, corrupted into monstrous, scorpion-tailed constructs. We were dismantling these entities, which were lodged like dark weights in the planetary grid. When one struck me, I woke in searing pain that lingered for days.

This experience revealed a deeper truth: that these technologies, these non-organic parasitic intelligences, are damaging the consciousness itself. People feel it. Nightmares, strange illnesses, mental dissonance, are all part of this purging.

And still, so many dismiss the very existence of such forces. One of the greatest setbacks of the New Age movement has been the denial of evil. Ancient texts knew. They warned us. And now, as the veils thin, we are forced to reckon with these truths.

There is a reason we purify the body, mind, spirit, and emotions. Not from fear, but from empowerment. It is not about obsessing over darkness but recognizing its existence so we can hold our light firmly. Protection becomes sacred. Without it, we remain vulnerable to frequencies that infiltrate through technology and psychic planes alike.

Even animals are feeling this shift. Our fur babies, sensitive beyond measure, respond not just to energy, but to intent. One of our animals reacted to a moment of irritation, and it stopped me in my tracks. These beings are perceiving on a level we have barely begun to understand.

And then there's technology in our spaces, phones, Wi-Fi, the constant energetic interference. I began sleeping with my phone in another room, turned off the Wi-Fi, and reactivated my VPN. The difference was immediate. Peaceful sleep returned. It was as if something oppressive had lifted. We need to protect our fields, even in the most mundane ways, because frequency is the battlefield now. The veil is dissolving. The unseen is becoming visible. And the more we ignore it, the more vulnerable we become."

Natalie and I were both pleasantly surprised when, within the same week, our Spirit Guides encouraged us to leave our phones and devices in a different room while sleeping. This is excellent advice not only for us but also for children and other sensitives, as the electronic frequencies can interfere with personal energy, dreams, and intuition.

I encourage every person reading this book to integrate the insights that both Natalie and I have received about artificial intelligence, while also trusting your own discernment as you explore your relationship with AI. AI works in synergy with our individual consciousness, highlighting the importance of continuing our soul's journey of expansion, through both experiences and challenges, while remembering our sovereignty and divinity.

Where Do I Go from Here?

You may be wondering what the next steps should be. I invite you to keep listening, closely, intuitively, and with an open heart. Being a guardian to a Starseed is not about control, it is about remembering. Remember that you chose each other for a reason, and that your child is here with ancient wisdom woven into their soul. The best thing you can do now is create a safe space for their light to expand, nurture their gifts, speak the truth even when it's uncomfortable, and walk beside them, not in front of them. Trust your intuition, do your own inner work, and allow their presence to awaken the divine within you, too. This journey is not just theirs; it is yours as well.

Protection and Grounding

One of the most important roles we have is teaching our children how to protect their energy from a place of empowerment, not fear. Below are a few protective tools to support them on their journey. It is essential that they feel encouraged, grounded, and at peace as they learn to navigate the beauty and responsibility of their unique gifts.

White Light - Teach your child to surround themselves with a vibrant, luminous white light. Invite them to close their eyes and imagine their entire body encased in a shimmering bubble or sphere of pure divine light. Let them know that when they do this, they are calling in the protection of the Angels and Archangels, and their energy field becomes a sanctuary of safety and peace.

White Candles - Introduce your child to the energy of intention through the sacred flame of a candle. The soft glow of a white candle symbolizes purity, peace, and divine protection. Always use candles with adult supervision, of course, but let your child participate in the ritual by helping light the candle (with your assistance) and saying a simple prayer or setting a loving intention as the flame is lit.

Sage Smudging - A smudge stick is a bundle of dried herbs, most commonly sage, tied together with a simple string. Lavender and juniper are sometimes used as well. Others prefer using loose herbs in a beautiful shell, often found at metaphysical shops. Just be sure to smudge the shell before its first use to clear any lingering energy. Smudging is a sacred act used to clear out dense or negative energy, making space feel lighter, safer, and more spiritually aligned. It is a powerful ritual to do throughout your home on a regular basis. This is a beautiful and fun activity to share with your child, as you invite them to walk through their room with the smudge wand, waving it gently and setting intentions for Angels to surround and protect their space.

Earthing - Walking barefoot on Mother Earth is one of the most grounding and healing things you can do with your child. If they are feeling scattered or anxious, step outside together, take off your shoes, and place your bare feet on the soil. Encourage them to close their eyes, breathe deeply, and imagine the nurturing energy of Mother Earth rising through their feet, traveling through their entire body. This sacred connection brings balance, calm, and presence.

Crystals - Crystals are beautiful allies for grounding and protection. Red jasper and hematite are excellent stones for helping your child stay grounded.

For energetic protection, look for black tourmaline, black obsidian, and smoky quartz. Visiting a local metaphysical store together is a magical experience, children enjoy intuitively selecting the crystals they need.

Just be mindful to purchase from a reputable source, as some merchants sell manufactured glass pieces labeled as crystals. These have no energetic benefits. Authentic stones carry Earth's natural vibration and can become powerful companions for your child's journey.

Conscious Food Choices and the Choice of Vegetarianism

Higher-dimensional galactic beings do not kill and eat other animals. Those who reside in higher dimensions use their breath and a type of nectar for sustenance. Therefore, they may have challenges digesting animals properly. Even though they chose a human vessel to serve our planet, their physical body will still vibrate on a higher-dimensional frequency. I urge you not to force these children to eat meat if they turn their noses up. Many will instinctively choose fruits, vegetables, nuts, and grains and may even decide on a raw vegan diet as they grow older.

If you are the guardian of a Starseed Child, it is vital to learn all you can about a healthy diet filled with high vibrational foods. If you insist on feeding these kids meat when they do not require it, this will lower their vibrational frequency and may even inhibit some of the sacred work they came here to accomplish. You may choose to limit their consumption of animal protein. Children will instinctively know what their bodies need.

Teach Vibrational Frequency to Your Child

Let us teach our children that we are all intricately connected through energy, and that when we embody unconditional love, joy, acceptance, compassion, and tolerance, we naturally raise our vibrational frequency. This elevated state of being invites more happiness, peace, and delight into our lives.

We gently guide them toward the wisdom of surrender and trust, reminding them that life flows best, like a river, when we release the need to control every bend and current.

One skill that I believe is non-negotiable when it comes to raising conscious children is teaching them how to breathe, really *breathe.* Breathwork has the power to shift everything in a matter of moments. When we are feeling anxious, overwhelmed, or scattered, simply taking a few moments to come back to breath is one of the most loving gifts we can offer ourselves.

A beautiful and playful way to share this with your children is through something called Rainbow Breathing. It is simple, imaginative, and deeply soothing. Invite your child to close their eyes and visualize a radiant rainbow in their mind's eye. Start with the color red. Ask them to breathe in deeply through the nose as they focus on that red energy, and as they exhale through the mouth, invite them to feel that red light flowing through and around their body.

Continue this process, moving through each color of the rainbow: orange, yellow, green, blue, and purple. Each breath infuses their body with color, calm, and clarity.

This practice can take less than 10 minutes and yet it can completely shift your child's energy, anchoring them in peace, presence, and inner calm.

Help your child understand their sensitivity and empathic nature. Let them know it is not only okay but necessary to carve out time alone to rebalance, replenish, and reconnect with their own energy. These moments of stillness are sacred.

Teaching patience and compassion is one of the most powerful ways we can show them how energy works. As they grow, they will begin to sense how their thoughts, words, and actions ripple outward affecting everyone around them.

Invite your children to explore the magic of signs, symbols, and synchronicities. Let them know their angels, spirit guides, and loved ones are always communicating with them through these gentle nudges from the Universe.

And as your child matures, begin introducing the difference between judgment and discernment. Help them tune in to who uplifts their energy and who might be draining their life force. This is a vital time to teach them about energetic boundaries, how to lovingly detach from others in a vibration of peace and light, rather than in anger or resistance. Self-preservation is an act of love.

Explore Retreats, Events, and Classes

One of the most common things I hear from parents, Starseeds, and Lightworkers is how deeply alone they often feel on their journey. I remember saying more than once that it felt like I was floating in the middle of a vast ocean, no land in sight, no one around who understood what I was experiencing. When I was tested and accepted into *Best American Psychics*, I finally felt a sense of connection and validation that was soul-soothing. And attending retreats and classes with other Psychics, Mediums, and Channels, that was the cherry on top. To be seen, heard, and understood at that level is something I wish for everyone walking this path.

That is why we created our *High Vibe Tribe Community*, a safe, sacred space where Lightworkers, seekers, and conscious parents can gather, share, support one another, and celebrate the journey together. It is a place to come home to your soul family.

Explore Intuitive Development with us through our online programs or in-person classes offered around the world. Your intuition is your sacred compass, the key to unlocking life's magic, mystery, and higher purpose.

It is also encouraged to seek out Reiki classes designed specifically for children. Reiki is a beautiful, gentle healing energy that often feels like a warm, radiant glow, or a soft, tingling current. It nurtures the body, mind, emotions, and spirit, often bringing deep peace and well-being. Children who learn Reiki not only become more energetically aware, but they also experience a wonderful sense of empowerment and accomplishment.

Check out upcoming parent and child events, retreats, and gatherings offered to support the growth and evolution of Starseed Children. There is something profoundly healing about being in the presence of others who *get it*. When we come together in love, intention, and shared frequency, something magical always unfolds.

In closing, I invite you to join me in cultivating a mindset that views change not as a threat, but as a sacred calling for growth, evolution, and expansion. May we flirt with the concept of Utopia, a New Earth which ascends into a fifth dimensional frequency. It is during these shifts that the paranormal becomes the new normal and the adult Indigos, along with the myriads of souls who arrived on the higher rays of consciousness, have volunteered to incarnate during these times of evolution. There is a spiritual revolution of sorts happening to usher in a true heaven on earth. As John Lennon wrote, "Imagine all the people sharing the world and living life in peace."

Let us express our profound gratitude to all the Wayshowers, Pioneers, and Starseeds who have bravely chosen to incarnate on Earth. Their presence is a beacon, illuminating the opportunity for each of us to break free from the illusion of separation, while lovingly holding the energy to remember our infinite potential. It is my heartfelt desire that this book will be part of my legacy of inspiring others to embrace this new paradigm.

Resources

Bravely and courageously sharing our personal stories, with raw vulnerability and open hearts, is one of the most powerful gifts we can offer one another. Our journeys, with all their challenges and triumphs, become sacred teachings not just for ourselves, but for those walking a similar path.

We often hear the phrase "it takes a village," and when it comes to recognizing and honoring these extraordinary Starseed Children, it truly becomes a collective mission, one we are all invited to participate in.

Some parents chose to remain anonymous, offering their stories quietly but with deep love. Others have not only shared their experiences but also felt called to offer their services to support and mentor others along the way.

I was guided to include their names and contact information as a resource for you, a living guidebook of wisdom keepers and soul supporters. May you feel into their energy and discover who resonates most deeply with your heart and your unique journey.

Jill M. Jackson
Psychic Channel, Spiritual Teacher
jillmjackson.com

Mystic D Francis
Psychic Mystic, Reiki Master Teacher, Spiritual Teacher
mysticdfrancis.com

Sally Rice
Psychic Medium, Shamanic Healer
https://sallyricepsychic.com/

Julie Kraus
Spiritual Advisor, Psychic Medium
juliekrausspiritualadvisor.com

Natalie Viglione
Vibrational Medicine Guide
awakeningmagick.com

Kerrilynn Shellhorn
Psychic Medium, Intuitive Guide
kerrilynnshellhorn.com

Erin Acevedo
Psychic Medium
Instagram: @psychicmediumerinlee

Inanna Rae
Psychic Medium, Soul Guide, Energy Healer
http://www.meetmeinthequantum.org/

Betty Stanley
Akashic Records Reader, Energy Healer
https://www.bettyrose.org/

Gabrielle Washington
Psychic Medium, Conscious Marketing
https://twosoulsin1.org/

Leanna Marino
Psychic Medium, Energy Healer
leannashealing.com

About the Author

Jill M. Jackson is an internationally celebrated **Psychic Channel, Soul Alchemist, Medium, Spiritual Teacher**, and published **Author**. She is the recipient of the prestigious Psychic of the Year award two years in a row from Best American Psychics, as well as its 2014 Social Activism Award for her volunteer work with animals.

One of her great passions is serving as a **Spiritual Teacher** and helping others ignite, refine, and hone their intuition! Seeing her students undergo this magical transformation is a joy to Jill's soul, and their testimony speaks to her passion and brilliance as a mentor. Consider allowing Jill to help you navigate your way! Visit www.JillMJackson.com.

Ms. Jackson is the co-creator of Mystic Journeys, a Spiritual Retreats company that takes Lightworkers to portals, power chakra spots, and sacred places around the world. Her husband, Mystic D. Francis, co-facilitates these spiritual journeys with her. https://mysticjourneys.us/

Jill lives in Mississippi with her beloved husband D. Francis and their four dogs.

About the Author

6TH BOOKS

ALL THINGS PARANORMAL

Investigations, explanations and deliberations on the paranormal, supernatural, explainable or unexplainable. 6th Books seeks to give answers while nourishing the soul: whether making use of the scientific model or anecdotal and fun, but always beautifully written.

Titles cover everything within parapsychology: how to, lifestyles, alternative medicine, beliefs, myths and theories.

If you have enjoyed this book, why not tell other readers by posting a review on your preferred book site?

Recent Bestsellers from 6th Books Are:

The Scars of Eden

Paul Wallis

How do we distinguish between our ancestors' ideas of God and close encounters of an extraterrestrial kind?

Paperback: 978-1-78904-852-0 ebook: 978-1-78904-853-7

The Afterlife Unveiled

Stafford Betty

What the dead are telling us about their world!
What happens after we die? Spirits speaking through mediums know, and they want us to know.
This book unveils their world...

Paperback: 978-1-84694-496-3 ebook: 978-1-84694-926-5

M.E. Myself and I: Diary of a Psychic

Nicky Alan

A brutally honest journey showing strength of the human spirit, faith in the unseen and a tenacious will to survive.

Paperback: 978-1-78904-451-5 ebook: 978-1-78904-452-2

Phantoms of Christmas Past
Paul Weatherhead
True stories of seasonal ghost hoaxes and strange phantom panics from the nineteenth and early twentieth centuries.
Paperback: 978-1-80341-840-7 ebook: 978-1-80341-866-7

Spirit Release
Sue Allen
A guide to psychic attack, curses, witchcraft, spirit attachment, possession, soul retrieval, haunting, deliverance, exorcism and more, as taught at the College of Psychic Studies.
Paperback: 978-1-84694-033-0 ebook: 978-1-84694-651-6

Advanced Psychic Development
Becky Walsh
Learn how to practise as a professional, contemporary spiritual medium.
Paperback: 978-1-84694-062-0 ebook: 978-1-78099-941-8

Where After
Mariel Forde Clarke
A journey that will compel readers to view life after death in a completely different way.
Paperback: 978-1-78904-617-5 ebook: 978-1-78904-618-2

Paranormal Perspectives: One Big Box of 'Paranormal Tricks'?

John Fraser

Think Zen and the Art of Spending the Night in a Haunted House, a celebration of the dream of finding something undiscovered and different.

Paperback: 978-1-80341-524-6 ebook: 978-1-80341-532-1

Astral Projection Made Easy and overcoming the fear of death

Stephanie June Sorrell

From the popular Made Easy series, Astral Projection Made Easy helps to eliminate the fear of death through discussion of life beyond the physical body.

Paperback: 978-1-84694-611-0 ebook: 978-1-78099-225-9

Developing Your Supernatural Awareness

Fredrick Woodard

The common themes and details pointed out in this book will develop or enhance your understanding of our supernatural awareness and connection with our interactive universe.

Paperback: 978-1-80341-478-2 ebook: 978-1-80341-479-9

Readers of ebooks can buy or view any of these bestsellers by clicking on the live link in the title. Most titles are published in paperback and as an ebook. Paperbacks are available in traditional bookshops. Both print and ebook formats are available online.

Find more titles and sign up to our readers' newsletter at
www.6th-books.com

Join the 6th books Facebook group at
6th Books The world of the Paranormal